Amulets &
Talismans
for Beginners

T0275234

Richard Webster has written dozens of books on a wide variety of New Age subjects, from the psychic powers of pets to the ancient mysteries of feng shui. He has been a teacher, writer, and practitioner in the psychic world for most of his life.

Richard Webster lives in New Zealand with his wife.

Amulets & Talismans
for Beginners

*How to Choose,
Make & Use
Magical Objects*

Richard Webster

2004
Llewellyn Publications
St. Paul, Minnesota 55164-0383, U.S.A.

FIRST EDITION
Eighth Printing, 2022

Cover design: Ellen Lawson

Llewellyn Publications is a registered trademark of Llewellyn Worldwide Ltd.

Library of Congress Cataloging-in-Publication Data

Webster, Richard, 1946–
    Amulets & talismans for beginners: how to choose, make & use
magical objects / by Richard Webster
        p. cm.
    Includes bibliographic references (p.) and index.
    ISBN 978-0-7387-5246-4-7
    1. Amulets. 2. Talismans I. Title: Amulets and talismans for
beginners. II. Title.
    BF1561.W43 2004
    133.4'4—dc22   2003060510

Llewellyn Worldwide Ltd. does not participate in, endorse, or have any authority or responsibility concerning private business transactions between our authors and the public.
    All mail addressed to the author is forwarded, but the publisher cannot, unless specifically instructed by the author, give out an address or phone number.
    Any Internet references contained in this work are current at publication time, but the publisher cannot guarantee that a specific location will continue to be maintained. Please refer to the publisher's website for links to authors' websites and other sources.

Llewellyn Publications
A Division of Llewellyn Worldwide Ltd.
2143 Wooddale Drive
Woodbury, MN 55125-2989
www.llewellyn.com

Printed in the United States of America

Other Books by Richard Webster

Astral Travel for Beginners

Aura Reading for Beginners

Dowsing for Beginners

Feng Shui for Beginners

Soul Mates

Spirit Guides and Angel Guardians

Numerology Magic

101 Feng Shui Tips for the Home

Palm Reading for Beginners

Seven Secrets for Success

Success Secrets: Letters to Matthew

Practical Guide to Past-Life Memories

Write Your Own Magic

Pendulum Magic

Is Your Pet Psychic?

How to Write for the New Age Market

For our grandson
Blake Jamie Martin

Contents

introduction

WHEN I WAS growing up, my family spent every summer vacation at a beach resort. My sister Penny became good friends with a farmer who lived nearby named John. Every day she would help him milk his cows, and gradually we all got to know him. One day I commented on an unusual ring that he wore on the ring finger of his right hand.

"That's my mascot," he told us. "It's made from a horseshoe nail."

He took it off and allowed us to examine it. The nail had been hammered into the shape of a ring, creating an unusual piece of jewelry.

Penny wanted to know why he wore such a strange-looking ring. John looked embarrassed and rubbed the ring between his fingers.

"It protects me," he said. "Keeps me safe from harm."

"A lucky charm?" Penny inquired.

John shrugged his shoulders. "It's more than that. It's sort of a magic ring. It brings good things to me and protects me from the bad."

"How does it do that?"

John looked surprised and passed the ring back to my sister. "Can't you feel the energy in it?"

We passed the ring around again. This time we all felt that the ring possessed some strange power. John laughed at our looks of surprise.

"Don't you know that blacksmiths are magicians?" he asked. He took the ring back and rubbed it gently again before putting it back on his finger.

That was my first experience of handling a truly magical object. I resolved there and then that, one day, I would have a ring made from a horseshoe nail.

I did not know it at the time, but this was only the beginning of my journey into the ancient world of amulets, talismans, and lucky charms. In this book, I hope I can, like that farmer so many years ago, introduce you to this fascinating and life-changing subject.

There are many people today who think that we are much smarter than our ancestors, and that we know virtually everything that needs to be known. We conveniently forget that over the course of history we have forgotten much more than we have ever learned, and that our "primitive" ancestors functioned extremely well in the worlds they lived in. Many of the secrets of their success, so to speak, are lost to us today. What wisdom, for example, was locked away in the hundreds of thousands of scrolls in the library of Alexandria, or in the Temple of Jerusalem, or at Ptah in Memphis? We simply do not know.

We do know that our ancestors were highly intelligent people who delighted in knowledge and learning, and just a few examples of the fruits of their labor bear this out. Three hundred years before the birth of Christ, the Greek mathematician Bratosthenes determined the circumference of the globe and was only 202 miles off. (The belief that the world was flat came many hundreds of years later.) Moschus the Phoenician was aware of the atom and declared that it was divisible. The enormous harbor that Herod the Great built at Caesarea Maritima had a breakwater that was more than 197 feet wide—a wonder of engineering by any standard. Alexander Flinder, the coordinator of excavations at the harbor wrote, "This Herodian port is an example of a twenty-first century harbour built two thousand years ago".[1] The Romans were able to make a form of cement that hardened under water, something that was later lost and reinvented in the Middle Ages.[2] The Celts had a reaping machine that was lost and reinvented in the nineteenth century.[3] The Hindus were performing complex plastic surgery two thousand years ago.[4] The Chinese had discovered and were using aluminum fifteen hundred years before it was rediscovered in 1827.[5] Clearly, our ancestors did much more than fumble about in primitive premodern darkness.

We also know that people from ages past believed all sorts of things that are often no longer accepted by educated people today. For instance, they believed that certain objects contained incredible power and energy and could be used to assist them in all manner of endeavors and protect them from every conceivable danger. These objects—amulets, talismans, and lucky charms—played significant roles in the lives of people of earlier times. Modern-day people, however, scoff and would never use such things. Or would they? Today, more people than ever before are wearing items such as St. Christopher medals, ankhs, crucifixes, and signs of the zodiac, to name only a few. All of these are charms, amulets, or talismans. Much of the time, the people wearing them have no idea what these objects are. They may even consider them to be nothing more than attractive fashion accessories. Even so, they are still receiving some of the benefits that come from using something that contains magical power.

In truth, amulets, talismans, and lucky charms are as important to many today as they were hundreds or even thousands of years ago—it's just that sometimes this importance is not immediately apparent. Even people who express no interest—or actively express disbelief—in the subject use amulets, charms, and talismans. Few people would pass a four-leaf clover without picking it. Many athletes have "lucky socks" or other items of apparel that cannot be washed until the season is over, in case the magical power they possess is lost. An actor I know will not go on stage unless he is wearing a certain pair of underwear that provides him with luck. He would not like to be told that these could be considered a talisman or good luck charm, but, in fact, that is exactly what they are.

I hope I have confirmed what you must already have known intuitively when you picked up this book: the objects we instinctively keep near us for comfort, protection, luck, or assistance have considerable power—power that has been known to man for millennia. This book will help you understand not only the sorts of amulets, talismans, and lucky charms we encounter every day, but it will guide you as you create objects that can be fine-tuned for your own needs and desires. Along the way, you'll learn much of the rich history of amulets and talismans and the famous magicians who have created and used them. Amulets, talismans, and lucky charms can have a very real effect of your well-being, and I hope, with the help of this book, that they will soon be a beneficial part of your life.

what are they?

PEOPLE FREQUENTLY USE the words "talisman," "amulet," and "lucky charm" interchangeably. This is not correct, but it is easy to see how the confusion arises, as the dividing line between them is frequently hard to define. This chapter will help you understand the subtle distinctions between the three.

Talismans

Talismans are objects designed to give specific power, protection, encouragement, and energy to those who wear or own them. The important thing to note is that talismans always provide *specific benefits* to their owners and are usually made for specific purposes.

Talismans can be made from almost any material, though they are frequently made of metal, stone, or parchment and are inscribed with words or pictures. They are often made at spiritually and cosmically significant times to help provide power and energy that can be used by whoever owns them. The most powerful ones are actually made by their owners. Although they can be created for both positive and negative purposes, it would take an extremely brave—and foolish—person to make a negative talisman deliberately.

History is full of examples of talismans at work. Catherine de Medici, for instance, wore a specially made talisman that gave her power and the gift of clairvoyance. It was formed from several metals mixed together at auspicious astrological times. One side of this talisman depicted the god Jupiter, the eagle of Ganymede, and a demon with the head of Anubis, an Egyptian god. The other side contained a picture of Venus, flanked by demons. It is believed that the Venus is actually a portrait of Catherine de Medici, because many talismans are in the form of a disc, one side of which depicts the owner, while the other illustrates whatever it is that he or she desires. Catherine de Medici's talisman was destroyed when she died, but a copy can be found in the Bibliothèque nationale de France in Paris.

Talismans are common even today—even if their users don't acknowledge them as such. People engaged in competitive activities frequently use items of clothing as a talismans to improve their performances. Vida Blue is an excellent example. Blue was a famous baseball pitcher in the 1970s and 80s. He believed that his cap brought him luck and made him pitch better. Consequently, for several seasons, he never went to the mound without that exact cap. After a number of years, the hat finally became so filthy and faded that league officials told Blue that he would be suspended if he did not change hats. Blue agreed and held a pregame ceremony to burn his old hat before putting on the new one. (Blue probably didn't know it, but he was using an ancient rite to say goodbye to his talisman.)

In Hong Kong, I have seen people who keep photographs and drawings of books and computers in their wallets and purses to help them become more academic. I also know someone who keeps a photograph of Jesus in his wallet. He has frequent eye problems, and carries the picture, even though he is not a Christian, because Jesus was known to heal the blind.

Talismans have also come in various natural forms. The earliest talismans were natural. Primitive people frequently used objects made from parts of animals. An eagle's feather, a shark's tooth, or a leopard's claw provided power and prestige to the wearer. A necklace made from the teeth of a predatory animal is another good example. This was intended to provide not only protection, but also to give the wearer some of the qualities of the animal the teeth originally belonged to. Someone wearing a necklace made from a beaver's teeth would become industrious, while someone wearing a shark's tooth would become strong, fierce, and energetic, for example.

Amulets

Unlike talismans, amulets are intended for more general purposes and usually provide protection from danger. They can also ward off illness and ill fortune. While talismans are active, amulets are passive, reacting to events in the wearer's life rather than specifically creating something. (We expect amulets to provide protection, but occasionally the opposite occurs, and the amulet actually makes life more dangerous. The most famous example of this is the Hope Diamond, which caused misery and grief to everyone who owned it.)

Originally, amulets consisted of natural objects. "Lucky" rabbits' feet and four-leaf clovers are examples of such amulets. It wasn't long, though, before manmade objects became amulets, especially in the forms of various body adornments. Jewelry is still frequently used as an amulet.

An amulet can also be a specially made object you carry with you for protection. For example, St. Jude is considered the patron saint of policemen, and in the early twentieth century, many police officers in New York carried St. Jude medals with them to provide protection.

Lucky Charms

Lucky charms combine the qualities of both amulets and talismans. They are active like talismans and generalized like amulets. Charms are intended to attract good luck and good fortune to whoever owns them.

Originally, charms consisted of words that were either spoken or sung. The word "charm" itself is derived from the French word *charme*, meaning "song." The blessing that a priest gives at the end of a church service is an excellent example of a traditional charm. When people began writing the words down rather than saying them, charms became associated with magical objects like amulets and talismans.

People have used lucky charms to provide protection and attract success for things other than themselves. In 1968, contractors working on the Vanguard rocket project for the United States Navy said a succession of failures was caused by the absence of St. Christopher medals on the rockets. St. Christopher is widely considered to be the patron saint of travelers, and medals imprinted with his image are thought to protect people as they travel. A medal was attached to the next rocket, and it performed perfectly.[1]

John's horseshoe ring mentioned in the introduction is also a good example of what I mean by lucky charm. It protected him, but it also brought good luck to him. (Incidentally, though it is not easy to find a blacksmith these days, it is well worth the effort. When you find one, ask the blacksmith to make you a ring from a horseshoe nail. You will then own an unusual object that will attract good luck and provide protection against evil. A ring of this sort is the most effective lucky charm I have ever come across.)

As you can see, it is sometimes difficult to say if a certain magical object is an amulet, lucky charm, or talisman. In fact, it is not at all unusual to find one object performing all three functions depending on the beliefs of its owner. Essentially, though, talismans provide active power; amulets provide passive protection; and charms attract good luck and provide protection from bad. It probably makes no difference, in the end, what you call them, just as long as you choose the correct object for your specific needs. What follows will help you do just that.

amulets

THE ANCIENT EGYPTIANS had four words that could be translated as "amulet." All of them come from verbs that meant "to guard" or "to protect." The Egyptians had amulets to help the living, and they also made funerary amulets to protect the deceased as they traveled through the underworld to heaven.[1] The word "amulet," as we English speakers know it, comes from *amuletum*, the Latin for "an act which averts evil." Another interesting derivation comes from the Arabic word *himalah*, which is the word for the cord that secures the Koran to the body. In much the same way, most amulets have been pieces of jewelry or other precious objects worn around the neck on a cord or chain.

Primitive people began wearing amulets because of a natural desire to protect themselves in the often-frightening world in which they found themselves living. Amulets provided them with protection for home, family, and livestock. They protected the user from enemies—natural or otherwise—and, most crucially, they provided protection from the evil eye (a subject on which I will comment at length shortly).

When the concepts of gods or a god became accepted, the gods were often credited with providing the protective qualities that amulets provided. This was not always the case, though. Different established and not-so-established religions also discouraged the use of amulets. It is hard to understand why, considering that amulets contain nothing inherently evil or anti-religious. Their purpose was and still is solely to provide protection for the wearer, and often they derive this protective power from the names of the gods who are inscribed on the amulets. Despite this, St. John Chrysostom and other Christian fathers denounced amulets because they were connected with magic.[2]

Governments also got in the act. In the later days of the Roman Empire, the emperor Caracalla became so concerned about the number of people wearing amulets that he issued an edict banning their use. Heavy penalties were inflicted on all who continued to wear amulets.[3]

In the fifteenth century c.e., however, the tide turned, and the Christian church began condoning amulets. The first of these was the cross, which was used to repel devils and disease-carrying spirits. This was followed by images of the Virgin Mary and the saints. Relics of the saints and martyrs were close behind, and, in time, the invention of the printing press enabled people to carry paper amulets and talismans.

The Evil Eye

Primitive man was fascinated with the eye for a number of reasons. The fact that different people had different colored irises was a source of fascination, as was the ability of the pupil to grow and contract in size. And it was possible to see a reflection of one's own image in someone else's eye. (This, by the way, is where we get the word "pupil," from the Latin, *pupilla*, meaning "small doll.") All of this lead primitive man to develop a healthy respect for the power of the eyes—a respect that has often turned to fear.

This mixture of respect and fear persists even now. Most people, for instance, are familiar with the expression "If looks could kill." Eyes are extremely expressive, and a hate-filled, envious, baleful, cold, or jealous stare can be highly intimidating. Recognition of the power of a look seems to transcend cultural and geographic boundaries. Not long ago, I witnessed a confrontation between people of different races, and people on both sides used the evil eye against their perceived enemies.

We all feel uncomfortable when someone fixes us with a hard stare, and most of the time we sense it even when someone is staring at us behind our backs. We also have the power to inflict the evil eye on someone else. When we deliberately stare at someone with negative thoughts in mind, we are doing it consciously. However, we can also do it unconsciously by staring too long at a person, animal, or object, perhaps with admiration or envious thoughts. Someone using the evil eye has the power to harm someone by a mere glance. The effects of the evil eye usually come from another human, but throughout history it has been believed that some reptiles and insects also possess this power to harm. (It is interesting to note that the word "ill" was originally a contraction of "evil eye."[4] This shows how convinced people were that the evil eye was able to physically harm and, even kill, others.)

HISTORY OF THE EVIL EYE

Belief in the evil eye is nearly universal and appears to date back to the dawn of history. Accounts of the damage that the evil eye creates can be found in Sumerian and Babylonian cuneiform clay tablets dating back to about 3,000 B.C.E. The Sumerian god Ea, for instance, waged constant war against the evil eye.

Since then, belief in the evil eye has spread around the world. Here are some of the words used to describe it in different parts of the world:

- Arabia–*ayn al-hasad*
- Armenia–*peterak*
- China–*ok ngan*
- Corsica–*innocchiatura*
- Ethiopia–*ayenat*
- France–*mauvais oeil*
- Germany–*böse Blick*

- Greece–*baskania*
- Haiti–*mauvais jé*
- Hungary–*szemverses*
- India–*drishtidosham*
- Iran–*aghashi*
- Ireland–*droch-shuil*
- Italy–*malocchio* (also *affascinamento* and *jettatura*)
- Netherlands–*booz blick*
- Norway–*skørtunge*
- Poland–*zte oko*
- Scotland–*bad Ee*
- South America–*mal de ojo*
- Spain–*mal de ojo*
- Syria–*aina bisha*
- Turkey–*nazar* (also *kem goz*)

Throughout history, different cultures have had unique and often highly nuanced beliefs associated with the evil eye and how to avoid its various effects. In India, Hindus believed in the power of the evil eye, possibly because the third eye of Shiva, the Destroyer, was believed to be able to destroy the entire universe with a mere glance. A Tamil proverb says, "It is better to be hurt by a stone than an evil eye."

The Egyptians used the *Udjat*, or Eye of Horus, as an amulet to protect them from the evil eye. Because the Udjat symbolized the eye of the sun god, it made an effective remedy to repel the weaker energies of the evil eye. Sometimes two eyes were used, and these represented the sun and the moon.

The ancient Hebrews believed in the evil eye and used the Star of David as protection from it. They also protected their children from the evil eye by passing them across the smoke of blessed candles.

At the end of the third century B.C.E., the Greek poet Apollonius of Rhodes wrote about the sorceress Medusa, who managed to destroy the giant Talos with a malicious stare. Apollonius wrote how Medusa bewitched the eyes of Talos with the evil in her own.

When the Roman historian Pliny the Elder wrote about the Triballi and Illyrii tribes, he explained how some of their members were able to kill others with their evil eyes. Pliny believed that one of the attributes of these people was double pupils in their eyes. Plutarch, Virgil, and Lucian also wrote about the evil eye.[5]

The Romans even went so far as to legislate against the evil eye, with the intention of punishing and banishing anyone who used it. Not surprisingly, this did not work, and in Italy today, people carry amulets depicting horns to protect them, as well as crucifixes and porcelain eyes.

The Hebrew Talmud says, "For every one that dies of natural causes, ninety-nine will die of the evil eye." Thousands of years later, Jewish people still say, "*kayn aynhorah,*" meaning, "May no evil eye harm you," to ward off the evil eye.[6]

The Bible also contains a number of references to the evil eye. In Deuteronomy 15:9 we find, "Beware that there be not a thought in thy wicked heart, saying, The seventh year, the year of release, is at hand; and thine eye be evil against thy poor brother, and thou givest him nought; and he cry unto the Lord against thee, and it be sin unto thee." Proverbs 23:6 is even more specific: "Eat thou not the bread of him that hath an evil eye, neither desire thou his dainty meats." Jesus specifically mentions the evil eye in Mark 7:22: "Thefts, covetousness, wickedness, deceit, lasciviousness, an evil eye, blasphemy, pride, foolishness: All these evil things come from within, and defile the man." Jesus also mentions the evil eye in the Sermon on the Mount (Matthew 6:22–23): "The light of the body is the eye: if therefore thine eye be single, thy whole body shall be full of light. But if thine eye be evil, thy whole body shall be full of darkness."

The early Christians, naturally enough, used a cross as a protective amulet against the forces of the evil eye. Even making the sign of the cross and saying a quick prayer was considered effective.

The evil eye is mentioned in the Koran, and readers are warned of its dangers. The Koran contains eight verses referring to the evil eye and gives advice on how to protect yourself and others from its negative effects. The Koran disapproves of charms and protective amulets, though, recommending instead that its readers seek the help and protection of Allah.

Belief in the evil eye was strong in ancient England and Ireland, as well. In Irish mythology, the story is told of Balor of the Evil Eye. One day, he happened to see druids preparing a potion for wisdom, and some of the concoction splashed onto his eye. This created an evil eye, which he kept closed when not engaged in battle. The eyelid was so heavy that he needed four assistants to open it. He was able to use this eye to petrify his enemies with a mere glance. Balor was eventually killed by his grandson, who put out the baleful eye with a slingshot.

In 1696, the English scholar John Aubrey published his *Miscellanies*, which contained information about the evil eye: "The glances of envy and malice do shoot also subtly; the eye of the malicious person does really infect and make sick the spirit of the other."

History is filled with examples of individuals and groups using the evil eye and being punished for it. The *Malleus Maleficarum* (literally, the "witch hammer"), the famous book for witch hunters published in Germany in 1486, mentions that certain people could bewitch their judges by a mere glance of their eyes. This was why many alleged witches were forced to walk backwards toward their judges. Countless people in medieval Europe were burnt to death because they were believed to possess the evil eye.

CATCHING THE EVIL EYE

Usually, the evil eye is passed on accidentally and is the result of either envy or praise. For example, it can be worrying if someone praises you or your children, as this could inadvertently cause harm to befall you or your family. In some cultures, the person giving the compliment would then spit three times to eliminate the possibility of accidentally passing on the evil eye.

It is even possible to turn the evil eye on yourself. If you became proud of something that you achieved and then experienced a sudden feeling of exhaustion, you may have done this. In Azerbaijan, they have a saying, "*Ozumun ozume gozum deydi*," which means, "I brought the evil eye on myself."[7]

In Italy, it is believed that some people are born with the evil eye and use it involuntarily. These people are known as *jettatores* ("projectors"). Their version of the evil eye is called *jettatura* ("projection"), in contrast to the accidental form created by envy or praise, which is known as *mal occhio* ("bad eye").

People with slightly unusual eyes were frequently accused of possessing the evil eye. In Palestine, it was believed that clean-shaven men with light-blue eyes were most likely to cast the evil eye. In some cultures, anyone who was different in any way was believed to have the evil eye. Someone unfortunate enough to be born with a clubfoot, for instance, might be regarded with suspicion, purely because he or she was different. Even a stranger would be regarded with suspicion, especially if he or she came from a different racial background.

PREVENTING THE EVIL EYE

In all of the cultures where some version of the evil eye appears, it is generally felt that children, pregnant women, and animals were most susceptible to the evil eye, but anyone could become a victim if they were not prepared. The evil eye is blamed, for example, for sudden attacks of diarrhea or vomiting, the drying up of milk in nursing mothers, and impotence in men.

Fortunately, different objects could be worn to avert the evil eye. Syrian and Palestinian women decorated themselves with blue beads, following the theory that like cures like.[8] Blue objects, particularly beads, have always been used to avert the evil eye. In Europe, malachite pendants with natural markings that resembled eyes were worn to protect the wearer from the evil eye. An amulet of reddish-brown chalcedony was engraved to show an eye in the center, surrounded by the deities that ruled each day of the week.[9] Today, a small amulet in the shape of an eye serves the same purpose. These are usually in the form of a pin or bracelet with the eye made of porcelain.

Hands have and continue to be used in many cultures to ward off the evil eye. Turning a hand into a fist and placing your thumb between the first and second fingers, allowing the thumb to protrude slightly is a powerful protection known as the "fig," "figga," or "fico" in various cultures. Pointing this at the person you suspect of giving you the evil eye will avert the danger. The fig symbolizes the male and female genitals, and it is believed that the potent, generative power this creates is easily strong enough to avert the evil eye. In Latin American countries, ebony figgas are worn as protective amulets, particularly by children.[10] Over the years, a number of people have told me how their thumbs subconsciously inserted themselves between the first and second fingers to create an impromptu protective amulet on occasions when they needed protection. Naturally, this can be done consciously, and you should do it whenever you find yourself in a stressful or potentially difficult situation.

In Italy, the "devil's horns" (*manu cornuto*) create an excellent remedy. These are created by bringing the two center fingers down to the palm of the hand and holding them in place with your thumb. This leaves the index and little finger raised to create the horns. It was not necessary to hold them upright. Merely holding the hand with the horns pointing downward is enough to avert the evil eye.[11] This gesture also protects men from impotency, one of the effects of the evil eye.

The Jewish people use their bodies to create a protective amulet against the evil eye. The thumb of the right hand touches the palm of the left hand, while the left hand thumb touches the right palm. The fingers are then closed around this arrangement and the person's chest, arms, and interlocked hands create a circle of protection.

There are two main cures for the evil eye in India, along with a host of lesser cures. The first main cure is to visit a temple or other holy place and pray to God. The second is to involve oneself in charitable undertakings. Another remedy is to burn camphor on a two-eyed coconut, wave it in the air, and then break it open. Alternatively, you can break open a lemon fruit, again after waving it in the air. Pieces of white pumpkin are traditionally strewn in the streets to frighten off the evil eye on important occasions, such as a housewarming party.

In Greece, they have a remedy that I have used myself to good effect. All you have to do is paint an eye in the middle of an attractive blue-colored ornament and then wear it as a necklace or bracelet. The fact that you are involved in creating the eye gives this amulet greater power. The Greeks are also likely to spit towards someone who pays them a compliment. This is believed to ward off the evil eye, which could reach you through a kind remark. Sometimes they spit three times because three is associated with the Holy Trinity. The Greek Orthodox Church recognizes the existence of the evil eye and recommends that only their priests be allowed to remove it, in case of demonic possession.

Small blue or black beads containing a black spot inside a white circle are a popular deterrent against the evil eye in Azerbaijan. They are called *gozmunjughu* and are usually worn as beads. Sometimes a single bead will be attached to a child's shirt. Larger versions of these are hung in people's homes. It is common to find large eyes at the entrances to commercial buildings. The McDonald's on Fountain Square in Baku is a good example.

Eye bead ornaments are also popular decorations in homes in Turkey. The eye is set in blue glass called *nazar boncugu* and protects the inhabitants of the house. Similar ornaments are also popular in Egypt. Originally, caravan men tied bands of these around the foreheads of camels before embarking on trips across the desert,[12] but now you frequently find them hanging from car mirrors and inside homes. They are also found on the clothing of small children.

In the West, we frequently pass compliments on other people's children, saying things like, "Hasn't he grown?" or "She looks darling." We think nothing of this, but in Egypt, remarks like these can terrify parents. If the words were said with malice or envy, the child would be harmed by the evil eye. Consequently, baby boys are sometimes dressed as girls, even to the extent of piercing their ears and giving them earrings to wear.[13] Sometimes, children are given ridiculous names to avert the evil eye. A boy might be given a girl's name, for instance. Because the evil eye is believed to harm food, young children are usually fed in private. In 1836, the British Egyptologist E. W. Lane commented on loving mothers deliberately leaving their children unwashed and wearing old clothing to mislead the evil eye. He wrote about encountering a beautifully dressed and charming woman, "and by her side a little boy or girl, her own child, with a face besmeared by dirt, and with clothes appearing as though they had been worn for months without being washed."[14]

Glass balls, known as Witch Balls, were used in the Americas as well as England to ward off the evil eye.[15] They were suspended in the windows of houses to attract the evil eye away from the occupants and to send the negativity back where it came from. Originally, Witch Balls were small green or blue balls of blown glass, full of different colored threads. The idea was that the evil eye would become so immersed in trying to unravel the different threads that its power would lessen. (Later, the balls became larger and used their reflective qualities to deflect the evil eye.)

In the East, carefully intertwined knots have been used to repel the evil eye. The idea behind this is that the evil eye would become so involved in the complexity of the knots that it would lose its force and power. It is possible that the complicated artwork of the Celts and Saxons was also devised with the idea of repelling the evil eye.

It is interesting to note that a number of things we take for granted today began as protection against the evil eye. Eye shadow, for example, had nothing to do with beauty initially. It was used to protect the wearer from the devastating effects of the evil eye. In the West, we often like to dress small girls in pink and boys in blue. This may seem to be nothing more than a charming custom, but, again, it was originally for protection. Boys were dressed in blue because blue was believed to ward off the evil eye, and this is also why, in the East, people still use strings of blue beads to adorn their children and livestock.[16] When the cord eventually breaks the child is considered old enough to withstand any future attacks of the evil eye.

In some cultures red is used to avert the evil eye. In India red cords are placed around the neck or wrists of young babies to provide protection. I understand this is also done in eastern Europe. In Italy, red coral amulets in the shape of an animal horn are worn by men.

Garlic cloves are another well known amulet and are considered good preventatives. Garlic is usually carried in a pocket for effective protection from the evil eye. Alternatively, cloves of garlic can be hung in your car, workplace, or house.

Eye-shaped amulets are the most common forms of protection, and they are normally blue in color and made of pottery or glass. Bracelets and necklaces of this color also provide protection. Eyes have been painted on the bows of boats for thousands of years to provide protection against the evil eye. This possibly began in Greece, as there is evidence that many triremes (ancient Greek warships) were decorated in this way more than two thousand years ago. Hand- and horseshoe-shaped amulets are also commonly used, often in combinations with eye amulets. Consequently, a powerful amulet might consist of an eye resting on the palm of a hand.

In his book, *The Evil Eye: A Folklore Casebook*, Professor Alan Dundes proposes that the evil eye causes living things to dry up. This results in mothers' milk drying up, people wasting away, fruit dying on the trees, unexplained weight loss, and impotence. In other words, the evil eye dries up liquids. As evidence of this, Professor Dundes says that belief in the evil eye began in Sumer and spread out in a circular direction, reaching as far as India to the east, Scandinavia and Britain to the north, Spain and Portugal to the west, and Northern Africa to the south. Belief in the evil eye reached South America with the Spanish conquest, and Indonesia with the spread of Islam.[17]

Famous Amulets

Certain amulets have stood the test of time and become well known because of the benefits they provide. Obviously, if these amulets had failed to produce the desired results, they would have been forgotten long ago. Anyway, wearing or carrying an amulet hurts no one, and a familiar, trusted amulet provides pleasure as well as protection.

ABRACADABRA

Today, the word "abracadabra" is usually considered a nonsense word used by conjurers. However, it was taken seriously in the Middle Ages, when people believed that it could cure fevers. These amulets were made of parchment, attached to linen thread, and worn around the neck. The word "abracadabra" was written in the form of an upside-down pyramid:

```
A   B   R   A   C   A   D   A   B   R   A
  A   B   R   A   C   A   D   A   B   R
    A   B   R   A   C   A   D   A   B
      A   B   R   A   C   A   D   A
        A   B   R   A   C   A   D
          A   B   R   A   C   A
            A   B   R   A   C
              A   B   R   A
                A   B   R
                  A   B
                    A
```

The idea was that when the person wrote down the word, dropping one letter in each row, until the word vanished, the ailment would disappear. Consequently, when worn as an amulet, it is important that it points downward. The triangular shape also symbolizes the Holy Trinity. Consequently, it is a powerful force against negative energies—one still in use today. A few days ago, I walked across a park and found that someone had written an upside-down pyramid in chalk on the concrete path. The word used to create it was "hangover." I'd love to know what effect the pyramid had on the writer's health.

Most of the time, this type of amulet is worn for nine days (nine being a sacred number) and then discarded, ideally by being tossed backwards over the left shoulder before sunrise into a stream that flows from west to east. There is much significance in this complicated procedure. The left side is related to the devil, and the amulet is disposed of before sunrise into a river flowing in the direction of the rising sun, all of which connects the banishment of evil by good to the rising sun that banishes darkness with light.

The origin of this amulet is unknown, but it became popular in the second century C.E. when the Cabalists began using it as a charm against evil spirits. The first written reference to it, with instructions on how to use it, was in a poem by Quintus Serenus Sammonicus, who was physician to Emperor Severus on his expedition to Britain in 208 C.E.

The meaning of the word "abracadabra" is unknown. One possible source of the word are the Aramaic words *Ab* (Father), *Bar* (Son), and *Ru'ach Acadach* (Holy Spirit). Another possibility is that it derives from the Hebrew word *Ha-b'rakah*, meaning "the sacred name." Yet another possibility is that it comes from Abraxas, a god whose image appeared on talismans and amulets worn by a Gnostic sect that followed Basilides of Alexandria. The letters of the Greek word "Abraxas" also symbolize the seven known planets. Abracadabra might also simply be the name of a demon. Ultimately, although there has been a great deal of speculation about the origins of abracadabra, no one knows for certain where it came from.

(Interestingly, abracadabra and hocus pokus, incantations commonly used by conjurers, both have Christian associations. Abracadabra can be translated as "Father, Son, and Holy Ghost" and hocus pokus comes from the

Latin, *hoc est corpus* which means "This is the body"—
that is, the body of Christ. Some magicians use an
extended version of the spell, "hocus pokus filiokus,"
which comes from *hoc est corpus filii*. This can be found
in the Catholic mass, and means, "this is the body of the
Son.")

ACORN

When I was a boy, I used to walk to school past a grove of
oak trees, and, as a result, I always had at least one acorn
in my pocket. I remember holding these in my hand during lessons—which means that they were acting as
amulets, even though I did not know the meaning of the
word at the time.

The acorn has been used as an amulet since druidic
times. The druids worshiped in sacred groves of trees,
and the holy Isle of Anglesey (off the coast of Wales) was
venerated because of the many groves of oak trees that
were found there. The druids celebrated an oak festival at
the time of the summer solstice on the twenty-first of
June every year.

Many other civilizations have venerated the oak and
its acorn. The oracle at Dodona in ancient Greece was
situated in an oak forest. The priests and priestesses
would listen to the sounds of the trees and interpret
them. The breezes in the branches were amplified by
large bronze vessels that vibrated in the wind.[18]

In Scandinavia, the oak is related to Thor, in India to
Indra, in Greece to Jupiter, and in Finland to Ukho. The

Romans made crowns of oak leaves to symbolize bravery and courage. The Old Testament speaks of the "diviner's oak" (RSV, Judges 9:37).

As well as being a protective amulet, the acorn is also considered a charm to attract good luck and a long life. Some people place acorns on window ledges to provide protection for the occupants of the house.

ANKH

The ankh is a cross with a loop instead of a vertical line on the upper half. It is sometimes called the key of life, as the gods of ancient Egypt are frequently depicted holding it by the loop, which makes it look like a key. I have also heard it described as being the cross of life. The Egyptians thought the ankh symbolized the eternal nature of life.

No one knows its origin. However, it is possible that it describes the union of male and female with the loop symbolizing the vagina, while the T-shape symbolizes the penis and testicles. Regardless of its origins, it has always been considered a powerful protective amulet that also provides good health and abundance.

BUTTONS

Today we consider buttons to be purely functional items, so it's hard to believe that buttons were in use for some fourteen centuries before buttonholes were invented. Buttons were originally considered to be both good luck charms and amulets, and they were exchanged as gifts.

Attractive buttons still make effective amulets, especially if they are given to you by someone who cares for you.

There are a number of superstitions about buttons. One I remember from my childhood is that it is considered bad luck to put a button in the wrong buttonhole accidentally. The remedy is to take the garment off completely and put it on again. Finding a button is considered fortunate and means that you will shortly make a new friend. Buttons even appear in black magic. If you are unwell and believe that the illness is caused by a bad spell, you should leave a black button where someone else will find it, and thus you pass the spell on.

CORAL

Coral is a hard calcareous skeleton secreted by anthozoan animals. Because it looks like the branch of a tree, coral is able to share in the symbolism of both water and trees. Red coral is also considered a sign of blood, which relates to life and ultimately the soul. The ancient Romans believed that red coral warded off evil spirits and the evil eye. This belief has lasted, and people still wear ornaments made of coral as amulets to protect themselves from the evil eye.

CROSS

Millions of people around the world wear a cross around their necks. In many cases, this is to tell the world that they are Christians, but other people wear them as protective amulets. The cross is one of the oldest symbols, and has been considered sacred for thousands of years. There are more than three hundred variations of the cross around the world, and many of these date from the Stone Age, showing just how old this symbol is. The Latin cross that symbolizes Christianity today was used by the ancient Egyptians and Phoenicians. The Greeks used it symbolize Bacchus and Apollo. Even temple prostitutes in ancient India wore it to symbolize life-affirming power.[19] The cross's origins are unknown, but it is possible that Coptic Christians took the much older Egyptian ankh and used it as a symbol to affirm the eternal life promised by Christ. The word "cross" comes from the Latin word *cruciare*, which means "torture." The word "crucifix" has the same source.

Christians began using the cross as an identifying symbol in the third or fourth century c.e. Originally, it depicted a lamb (the Lamb of God), rather than the human Jesus, on the cross. Crucifixes (depicting the human Jesus on the cross) were forbidden until the Council in Trullo finally approved them in 692 c.e.[20]

The Christian cross remained a symbol with no officially sanctioned powers, as the early Christians did not approve of amulets, for some time. It gradually became an amulet, though, when the church fathers decided to use the cross to encourage converts, particularly Celts, to consider the cross to be a symbol of Christ.

In the Middle Ages, people carried disk-shaped wax amulets of a lamb in front of the cross to prevent enchantments and a wide range of bad weather conditions. This amulet became known as the *Agnus Dei* ("Lamb of God"). It ultimately became so popular that a papal bull was passed in 1471, granting sole manufacturing rights to the pope. This amulet became—and continues to be—a highly lucrative source of revenue for the church.[21]

JADE

Jade has always been a popular amulet in China, possibly because vast amounts of jade are found there. People wear it to protect themselves from stomach aches and to become more fertile.

Green colored jade, in particular, has always been associated with fruitfulness and growth. Jade is also believed to assist women in childbirth. White jade, especially when made into an amulet with gold and ruby, is believed to protect the wearer from heart palpitations.[22] Businessmen in China would hold jade amulets while involved in important business transactions.[23] Today, jade amulets are used to protect the wearer from ill health and to encourage restful sleep and feelings of happiness and contentment. Jade is considered highly protective.

KNOTS

A belief that appears around the world is that knots can catch evil spirits. When I was growing up, I was fascinated with the series of knots that my grandmother had on all her kitchen aprons. She tied them for protection, both for her and for the food she was preparing.

A knot acts as a protective amulet that discourages evil spirits. Oddly enough, the clerical collar is derived from this. People thought that evil spirits could be caught up in the knot in the priest's tie, and consequently create mischief during church services. Turning the collar around made it impossible for priests to wear ties, and the problem was eliminated.[24]

Another religious reference to knots is the knotted fringe. The fringe confuses the evil spirits, while the knots trap them, and prevent them from causing any harm. Orthodox Jews take this several steps farther by knotting the fringe so that it spells out one of the unspoken names of God.

PARIK-TILS

Long before I saw a Native American medicine bag, I was familiar with *Parik-tils*, or blessing holders, used by Romany (Gypsies). These were small, drawstring pouches, containing a variety of small objects, such as coins, acorns, herbs, stones, feathers, and pieces of paper containing spells or words of wisdom. Anything at all could be placed into these bags, as long as they seemed appropriate for the purpose the bag had been made for. Bags could be made as amulets for protection against unseen forces, the evil eye, or any other form of negativity. Parik-tils can also be made as talismans to attract health, love, prosperity, and longevity. The finished bags were charged by passing them over a candle flame, before sprinkling them with water. A few drops of perfumed oil were added, and the amulet was ready to be worn.

Procuring Amulets

Traditionally, amulets were natural items. A dried vegetable, such as a red pepper, might be used, or an acorn, four-leaf clover, animal's tooth, or a semiprecious stone. However, anything that you personally like can be used as an amulet. You might choose a natural object, or you might prefer something manmade, such as a medal of a saint, a birthstone ring, a bell, key, pendant, or a drawing or photograph.

Take your time choosing a suitable amulet. Think about what you want it for, and how you will wear or carry it. Once you decide that you want an amulet for a specific purpose, a number of possibilities will quickly present themselves to you. I have seldom gone looking for a specific amulet, as usually the right object seems to find me. Some years ago, I got into conversation with someone at an airport, and when it was time for me to leave for my flight, the person I was chatting with gave me a small piece of hematite. This made a perfect amulet, as I was on my way to see a rather overbearing man about a business deal. The hematite protected me from his aggression and force.

You may choose to make your own amulets. *How to Make Amulets, Charms and Talismans* by Deborah Lippman and Paul Colin (M. Evans & Co, 1974) contains instructions on how to make many different amulets. The French philosopher Blaise Pascal is a well-known example of someone who made himself a protective amulet. He believed profoundly in the protective power of amulets, and always carried with him, sewn into the lining of his jacket, a sheet of paper containing a written message. He wrote this amulet after a distressing experience that occurred when the horses of his vehicle took fright when he was riding alongside the Seine river. The horses ran directly towards the river, but the reins broke just as they were about to pull Pascal's carriage over a precipice. The horses fell into the river, but a shaken and shocked Pascal and his wagon remained perched on the edge.[25]

Purifying Your Amulet

If you have purchased your amulet or received it as a gift, you will probably want to purify it before making use of its protective powers. This is because you will not know what undesirable energies it may have picked up before coming into your possession.

The traditional methods of purifying an amulet involve fire, earth, air, and water. Some people like to use all four, while others use just one. What you choose to do is up to you and is also partly dependent on the materials that make up the amulet.

Some people like to purify their amulets by creating a formal ritual. There is nothing wrong with this, and you may choose to purify your amulets in this way. Most people prefer to purify their amulets in a simpler, more casual manner. Although the process of purification can be fun, it is a serious task that should never be done flippantly.

Choose a time when you will not be disturbed and can focus on purifying your amulet. Although you can do this with like-minded people, it is usually better to do it on your own. I personally prefer to purify amulets outdoors, but have no objections to performing the ritual indoors if the weather is bad.

Here are some suggestions to help you decide on a method of your own.

FIRE

Purchase a white candle and pass your amulet through the flame. It is important that the candle has not been used for any other purpose beforehand, and it should be discarded once you have purified your amulet.

Also, on a sunny, cloudless day, you can place your amulet outdoors and allow direct sunlight to purify it.

EARTH

Bury your amulet in dry earth and leave it overnight. Alternatively, you may choose to place your amulet on the ground and leave it out overnight. This can be made more effective by surrounding the amulet with a circle of stones. Another method is to bury your amulet in salt for twenty-four hours. The salt should be discarded afterwards.

AIR

Purify your amulet in the air by facing east and holding your amulet as high as you can with both hands. Stand in this position for thirty seconds and then repeat by facing the south, west, and north directions.

Another method is to light a white candle and pass the amulet through the smoke. Incense can be used, if preferred.

You might also prefer to take several deep breaths, until you feel full of vibrant energy. Hold your amulet in your cupped hands and exhale over it.

WATER

Wash your amulet in running water. Tap water is sufficient, but it is better to wash your amulet in the water of a spring or stream. Allow the amulet to dry naturally in the fresh air.

If the materials in the amulet do not allow this, you can sprinkle a few drops of rain water over it. If necessary, immediately dry your amulet with a fresh towel.

Experiment with the different methods suggested here. Most of the time your amulet will let you know when it has been purified. You may experience a sudden sense of knowing that the task has been done. Alternatively, the amulet may feel different in some way. It might feel cleaner and fresher, for instance. If you receive no signs at all, purify your amulet again using fire, earth, air, and water, and then leave it for twenty-four hours before testing it again.

talismans

No ONE KNOWS how or when talismans were first devised. However, they probably date back to the Stone Age. Paintings on cave walls, such as the ones at Lascaux in France, show oxen, deer, and other animals. This was probably a form of sympathetic magic. By depicting animals on the walls of their caves, early people were using symbols to attract prey to them. From here, it is just a short step to creating a small object that could be carried around for the same purpose.

The first talismans were natural items, such as stones or bones, that happened to be of a shape that reminded the finder of a particular god or a particular ability or characteristic of a god or animal. Other items were crudely carved to represent various deities. As people became more skilled at making them, talismans gradually became more elaborate. Small carved figures of ivory, pottery and metal, dating from Paleolithic and Neolithic times still survive today. No matter how simple or detailed they happened to be, prehistoric people believed that talismans were imbued with the power of whatever it was they were made to represent.

Advanced ancient civilizations also used talismans. Excavations in Egypt, Chaldea, Persia, Greece, and Rome have all uncovered talismans. Instructions on how to make particular talismans have been found in Egyptian papyri. Not surprisingly, Greek and Roman talismans are closely associated with astrology, while Jewish talismans show the influence of the Cabala.

The Jewish *mezuzah* is a good example of an early talisman. It dates back to an instruction in Deuteronomy: "And thou shalt write them upon the posts of thy house, and on thy gates" (Deuteronomy 6:9). The mezuzah itself is a hollow metal tube that contains a sheet of parchment inscribed with the words "Hear, O Israel, the Lord our God is One." The mezuzah is nailed to the doorpost of the house, both consecrating and protecting it. The occupants kiss or touch the mezuzah whenever they pass it. Some people even carry mezuzahs around their necks. This is a recent practice. The original purpose of the mezuzah is to keep the home safe.

Talismans making use of sympathetic magic also persisted. Apollonius of Tyana, the first century C.E. Pythagorean philosopher, made a talisman to rid Antioch of scorpions. He buried a bronze model of a scorpion and erected a pillar over it. This talisman worked, and all the scorpions left Antioch.[1]

During the Crusades, many soldiers carried stones carved with runes to act as talismans. These rune stones had two purposes: to provide protection, and to ensure success in battle. Soldiers of this period also carried bloodstones with them. Bloodstone is associated with Mars, the god of war, and soldiers believed these stones would make them brave in battle as well as provide protection. They also believed that these stones could staunch bleeding, and they were frequently bandaged against wounds to help the healing process.[2]

It is interesting to think that jewelry worn purely for decorative purposes was not known prior to the time of the French Revolution. Before then, jewelry was worn for only two purposes: either to signify high social standing or as a talisman. Usually, the laws of the land forbade anyone who was not a member of the ruling class to wear jewelry. In the Middle Ages, for instance, people believed that wearing a ruby ring on the left hand would bring them land and titles, make them virtuous, and protect them from seduction. Naturally, a nobleman would not want any of his peasants to wear a ring of this sort.

Charging

The word "talisman" comes from the Greek word *teleo*, which means "to consecrate." Talismans are magical objects that must be endowed with their powers in some manner. In other words, talismans are *charged* to provide power and energy to enable them to achieve their tasks.

They are usually made and charged at specific times to provide them with the essential energies they need to do their specific work. Without charging, a talisman cannot perform its specific function.

Charging was (and still is) often done using a system of planetary correspondences that began in the Middle Ages. If, for instance, you created a talisman to attract money, you would probably empower it at one of the hours of Jupiter, as this planet is related to financial success. (I'll get to this system in greater detail shortly.) When the talisman is connected to the universal forces in this way, success is more likely to occur than would be the case if the timing were left to chance. Naturally, the person making the talisman needs to be fully focused on the desired end result the whole time he or she is working on it.

There are many different rituals associated with charging talismans. Many are incredibly complicated and difficult to perform. Some of these can be found in the works of famous occultists, such as Eliphas Lévi and Arthur Edward Waite. Eliphas Lévi wrote that, to charge a talisman, an altar with a tripod of sacred flame on it was required. Both altar and tripod had to be garlanded with specific colors determined by the days of the week. A carpet of a specific type had to be placed in front of the altar. On Mondays, for instance, this had to be a carpet made from lion skin. The person performing the ceremony had to wear robes of a specific color and also wear different kinds of jewelry, again determined by the day of the week. For instance, on Monday, a crown covered in yellow silk which had been embroidered with the Hebrew symbol of Gabriel in silver thread had to be worn. The robe for Monday required a collar that contained pearls, crystals, and selenite.

For most people, the cost of procuring all the required items would be prohibitive—to say nothing of the complexities of the actual ritual. Of course, at the time Eliphas Lévi was writing, much had to be deliberately concealed, and this may have been part of the reason for all the obstacles placed in the way of anyone wanting to practice magic. It is also possible that he did not want to give away too much information in a book, preferring to sell it to his private students.

Fortunately, you do not need to belong to a magical lodge or an esoteric order to charge a talisman, and there are a number of simple and highly effective ways to charge or consecrate your talisman, and I'll discuss them in detail in chapter 5.

PLANETARY CHARGING SYSTEM

This medieval method for charging talismans is not the quickest nor the most straightforward, but it does give you an excellent idea of what past magicians went through and the importance they placed on charging. See chapter 5 for other charging methods.

Before we go any further, we need to know something more about the medieval planetary system of creating and charging talismans. In medieval times, talismans were based on either the twelve signs of the zodiac or the known planets. However, because the planets symbolically rule the signs of the zodiac, they gradually replaced the signs, and most talismans are based more on the planets than the signs.

Before Uranus, Neptune, and Pluto were discovered, magicians and astrologers used seven planets (they considered the sun and moon to be planets). We still use these seven planets because of the immense amount of knowledge, mythology, and symbolism associated with each. There are other reasons as well. Seven has always been considered a highly spiritual number. For instance, God made the world in six days, and rested on the seventh. Seven is the sum of four and three, two other magical numbers, and is not divisible by any other number. When we talk of "the seven seas," we don't mean that there are just seven seas. We use the number seven to indicate completeness, or all of the seas.

Not surprisingly, there were also seven talismans, one for each day of the week. However, according to Albertus Magnus, the great thirteenth-century scholar and teacher of St. Thomas Aquinas, many people also had an eighth talisman that could be worn at any time. This talisman ensured that the wearer would triumph over his or her enemies.[3]

Primitive people considered the sun and moon to be the source of all life. In effect, they were the father and mother of the universe. Gradually, gods were attributed to the five visible planets and eventually a pantheon of gods developed to look after the affairs of mankind on earth. Each had specific duties and responsibilities, and in time the planets also became associated with particular qualities found in natural objects. People found that pairing similarly affiliated objects would increase their effectiveness. It was believed, for instance, that gemstones were more effective when combined with metals that shared the same temperament. Here is a list that the occultist Pierre de Scudalupis published in 1610 showing the affinities between the planets and the seven principal metals and precious stones.[4]

PLANETS	METALS	PRECIOUS STONES
Moon	Silver	Crystal
Mercury	Mercury	Lodestone, alectoria
Venus	Copper	Amethyst, pearl, sapphire, carbuncle
Sun	Gold	Sapphire, diamond, lodestone, jacinth
Mars	Iron	Emerald, jasper
Saturn	Lead	Turquoise and all the black stones

Although there have been a few minor alterations, his list can still be used today. A comprehensive modern-day list can be found in appendix A.

According to the medieval magi each planet is also associated with a specific day of the week.

- Sunday relates to the Sun.

- Monday relates to the Moon.

- Tuesday relates to Tiw, the old English variant of Tyr, the Germanic god of war. The Romans related him to their god Mars, and consequently, *dies Marti* (Mars' Day) became *Tyrsdagr* (Tuesday).

- Wednesday is named after Woden, and is ruled by Mercury.

- Thursday is named after Thor, the god of thunder. He can be related to Jupiter.

- Friday is named after Freya, the goddess of marriage. Not surprisingly, this is related to Venus.

- Saturday is named after the Roman god of time, Saturn.

The first hour of each day starts when the sun appears over the horizon. This hour is ruled by the planet of the particular day. Consequently, the first hour of Tuesday is ruled by Mars, and the first hour of Saturday is ruled by Saturn. The other hours of the day are dedicated to each of the planets in a specific order known as the Chaldean order of the planets.

Some five thousand years ago, Mesopotamia was occupied by the Chaldeans, a culture fascinated with astronomy and mathematics. Much of our knowledge of astrology and numerology can be credited to them. They noticed that the planets moved at different speeds, and the Chaldean order of the planets is based on each planets speed as it moves across the sky, starting with the slowest-moving planet and ending with the fastest: Saturn, Jupiter, Mars, the sun, Venus, Mercury, and the moon. This means that in the case of Saturday, we start with Saturn ruling the first hour, followed by Jupiter, Mars, the sun, Venus, Mercury, and the moon, before starting again with Saturn. In the case of Wednesday, which is ruled by Mercury, we start the first hour of the day with Mercury, followed by the moon, Saturn, Jupiter, Mars, and so on.

This sequence is easy to follow, and you will find it becomes automatic after you have used it for a while. However, it is made more complicated by the fact that day and night do not consist of exactly twelve hours each, all year round. Consequently, it is necessary to divide both day and night into twelve equal periods of time, which may be more or less than a true hour. In winter, when the days are shorter, the daytime hours will be less than sixty minutes, but the night-time hours will be longer. It is possible to obtain information about the rising and setting times of the sun in astrological almanacs. Many daily newspapers contain this information for your location, also. The different planetary days and hours show us the correct times in which to work on talismans for any purpose.

For example, then, if you wanted to charge a talisman to attract friends, you would probably charge it in the hours of Jupiter (and would use various symbols that represented that planet on the talisman) because Jupiter is, among other things, associated with friendship. Appendix A has a complete list of planetary correspondences. (We can take all of this a step further, by including the twelve signs of the zodiac, and a chart of zodiacal correspondences is also included in appendix A.)

Famous Talismans

Certain talismans have achieved fame because of their demonstrated potency and effectiveness. Consequently, it is not surprising that wonderful stories have been created about some of them.

AGLA

The letters *AGLA* are an acronym for the Hebrew words "Thou art mighty forever, O Lord." When inscribed on a talisman, the letters *AGLA* imbue the talisman with divine power. In the Middle Ages, talismans with this wording were used to ward off fever.

THE CHALICE OF THOTH

Despite its ancient-sounding name, the Chalice of Thoth is a comparatively recent talisman that has become popular because it is an effective talisman that is easy to prepare and use. Thoth was the Egyptian god of wisdom, learning, and magic. Not surprisingly, his name has been attached to many aspects of the occult. The famous twentieth-century magician and occultist Aleister Crowley even called the tarot deck the "Book of Thoth."

A chalice is a cup, and usually refers to the cup used to celebrate the Christian Eucharist. Paul refers to "the cup of blessing which we bless" in his first letter to the Corinthians (1 Cor. 10:16). In the Middle Ages, a legend began that claimed that the chalice used at the Last Supper was actually the Holy Grail. There have been many other possibilities suggested, but the one I find most intriguing is the one that suggests that the Holy Grail was actually Mary Magdalene herself. This legend says that she was secretly married to Jesus, and was pregnant at the time of his death. Consequently, she carried in her womb the Holy Grail. This association with both love and spirituality is likely to explain how this talisman obtained its name.

Throughout the world, the cup or chalice symbolizes love and spirituality. The Chalice of Thoth is intended to attract love and has the advantage of being easy to make and use. All you have to do is draw two identical chalices on a sheet of pink paper. Drawing them on pink fabric, especially silk, is even better. Cut the paper or fabric in two, and place one of these halves close to your heart and beneath your clothing. The other piece needs to be placed somewhere out of sight, close to where the object of your affection spends much of his or her time.

BELLS

Bells have been used as amulets and talismans ever since they were invented. In the Bible, we read that bells were attached to the hem of Aaron's robe to act as protective amulets (Exod. 28:33–35). Iron was considered the natural enemy of Satan, who was also believed to be frightened of the sounds that bells make. Consequently, the bells that summon people to church also frighten off Satan and his helpers.

For this reason, bells became popular personal talismanic devices in medieval times. They were attached to horses and children's toys to frighten away any evil spirits.

An eighteenth-century manuscript in the Bibliothèque de l'Arsenal in Paris describes how to make and use "the necromantic bell of Girardius." The bell has to be made from an alloy of lead, tin, iron, gold, copper, fixed mercury, and silver. It must be cast at the exact time of birth, on the birthday of the person who is to use it. A number of words are inscribed on the bell. The word "Jesus" is engraved on the ring which is used to attach the bell to its holder. Below this, on the outside surface of the bell is engraved the full date of the person who will be using it. One third of the way down the side of the outside of the bell is the word "Adonai." Below this are the symbols of the seven planets. Close to the base is the the tetragrammaton (see the entry below for an explanation of the Tetragrammaton). This bell then needs to be buried in the middle of a grave in a cemetery and left there for seven days. Once it has been dug up again, the bell can be used by its owner to make contact with the dead.

THE BLACK PRINCE'S RUBY

The Black Prince's ruby is a talismanic stone that I saw many years ago in the Jewel House at the Tower of London. In the fourteenth century, the Black Prince (Edward, Prince of Wales) was given this stone by Pedro the Cruel, king of Castille, who is believed to have murdered the king of Granada to obtain it. One hundred years later, King Henry V had the stone mounted in the coronet he wore at the Battle of Agincourt. During the battle, someone aimed a blow at the king's head. The coronet diverted the blow, but the part of the coronet that contained the ruby was cut off in the attack. Not surprisingly, it was believed that the talismanic nature of the ruby saved the king's life.

Evidence of this is that the king undoubtedly knew of the ruby's talismanic qualities. The ruby relates to Mars, the planet that rules warfare, and is believed to provide protection and success in conflict.

THE LEE PENNY

Sir Walter Scott's novel *The Talisman* was about a famous talisman called the Lee Penny. It was named after Sir Simon Lockhart of Lee, who attempted to take the heart of Robert the Bruce to the Holy Land but did not succeed. The legend says that Sir Simon received the talisman as a reward after releasing a high-ranking Saracen. However, although appealing, this story cannot be correct. The Lee Penny is a heart-shaped red stone, set inside a silver English groat. This was a common coin at the time of King Edward IV, who ruled from 1461 to 1483, almost two hundred years after the time of Sir Simon Lockhart.

The power and reputation of the Lee Penny was so great that in the seventeenth century, the burghers of Newcastle borrowed the coin to help them cure a plague of cattle. There is only one Lee Penny, and it is still owned by the Lockhart family in Scotland. The origin of its strange power is unknown.

SEAL OF SOLOMON (STAR OF DAVID)

Probably the most famous talisman of all is the Seal of Solomon. This is the familiar six-pointed star, created by two overlapping triangles. The triangle that points upward represents fire, the sky, and masculinity. The downward-pointing triangle represents water, earth, and femininity. The star created by combining these opposites provides ultimate universal protection for anyone who wears it. Consequently, it is possible that the famed turn-of-the-century occultist Arthur Edward Waite under-stated the power of this talisman when he wrote, "Nothing was believed impossible for those who possessed it [the Seal of Solomon], as it had power over all spirits, which is equivalent to saying it represented a strong psychic force."[5]

Around the world, this talisman is commonly known as the Star of David, and it symbolizes the Jewish religion as well as the nation of Israel.

The Seal of Solomon is commonly believed to date back to King Solomon, the son of King David, who lived in the tenth century B.C.E. Solomon is remembered mainly for his wisdom, but he was also an expert exorcist and magician. In fact, this talisman probably predates King Solomon by many hundreds of years, as ancient forms of it have been found in India.

In India, the Seal of Solomon symbolizes Vishnu, the second person in the Hindu trinity. (The others are Brahma and Shiva.) The sun is often placed in the middle of the two triangles, creating a powerful talisman that symbolizes all seven of the planets known to the ancients. In the West, the Tetragrammaton—the divine Hebrew name for God (see page 58)—is often inscribed in the center of a Seal of Solomon. The six points of the triangle denote Saturn, Jupiter, Mars, Venus, Mercury, and the moon.

The Theosophical Society, an organization dedicated to the concept of a universal brotherhood of humanity, adopted Solomon's Seal to indicate the importance of their work.

An interesting example of this talisman can be found in the Würzburg Museum, in Bavaria. The six-pointed star is crudely drawn on a piece of parchment, along with six characters, which may be astrological in nature. This talisman was found on the body of Count Anselm, bishop of Würzburg and an accomplished alchemist, after his death in 1749.

In the original Hebrew, the Star of David is referred to as the Shield of David. This is because the star shielded people from negative energies.

TETRAGRAMMATON

The Tetragrammaton was a popular talisman in the Middle Ages and was believed to protect the wearer from enemies and attract good relationships, peace, and a long life.

The Tetragrammaton, literally "the four letters" in Greek, is the four Hebrew consonants (either *JVHV* or *YWHW* depending on the transliteration of Hebrew to the Roman alphabet) that early Jewish writers used as a substitute for the unspeakable name of God. The unspeakable name may be derived from a Hebrew word meaning, "He that is and shall be," that served as a substitute for the unutterable name of God. The Tetragrammaton is often pronounced Yahweh or (more often, though incorrectly) Jehovah.

The talisman was usually made in the form of a pentacle, with the five syllables of the word "Tetragrammaton" inscribed in each corner.

THE HAND OF FATIMA

The Hand of Fatima is a powerful Arabic talisman, symbolizing generosity, hospitality, and the beneficial power of God. The Etruscans used the same symbol to represent justice and fair play. It is believed to have been rediscovered by the eighteenth-century Italian doctor and alchemist Count di Cagliostro in an old manuscript he found in the Castle of Saint Leon, in which its use as a double oracle was explained.[6]

Lady Fatima was a daughter of the prophet Mohammed. Her mother was Khadijah, the prophet's first wife. When she grew up, she married Ali, Mohammed's cousin, and they had three sons, Hasan, Husain, and Muhain. Because of her purity, Fatima was known as *Al-Batûl* (the clean maid or virgin), even after she became a mother. She was also known as *Al-Zahra* (bright blooming). Mohammed considered her to be one of the four perfect women. The others were his wife Khadija, Pharaoh's wife, and the Virgin Mary.

The Hand of Fatima talisman is comprised of the right hand (which is considered the hand of honor) with each finger representing a member of Fatima's family. The thumb depicts Mohammed, the first finger, Lady Fatima, the next depicts Ali, her husband, and the final two represent two of her sons, Hasan and Husain. The five fingers also symbolize the Five Pillars of Islam: to observe the fast of Ramadan, to make a pilgrimage to Mecca, to give alms to the poor, to perform the necessary ablutions, and to oppose all infidels.

The Hand of Fatima was drawn in a special way in medieval manuscripts (see illustration below). This later addition is of unknown origin, but became popular as it enabled people to indulge in some character analysis. The hand was divided into cells, with each cell containing a letter and corresponding number. A name could be translated into numbers and then the numbers could be analyzed based on a table of number associations (facing page). The examples below show how this works.

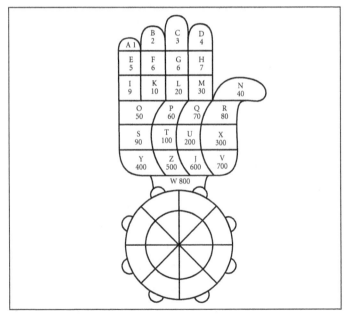

The Hand of Fatima

Number Associations

1	Passion, determination, success.	20	Disappointment, tears.
2	Death, disaster.	21	Ruthless, coarse, turbulent.
3	Intuition, mysticism.	22	Discreet, circumspect, inscrutable.
4	Knowledge, power, application.	23	Secrets, honorable, slow progress.
5	Love, wealth, happiness.	24	Apathy, conceit, selfishness.
6	Work, satisfaction.	25	Discernment, acumen, fruitful.
7	Thought, contemplation, innocence.	26	Beneficial, valuable, serviceable.
8	Love of truth and family values.	27	Braveness, determination, constant.
9	Pain, sorrow, reflection.	28	Tenderness, love, generosity.
10	Satisfaction, upward progress.	29	No reading.
11	Success after difficulty.	30	Marriage, long-term relationships, success.
12	Good fortune, stroke of luck.	31	Aspiration, determination, achievement.
13	Disbelief, cynicism, negativity.	32	Purity, modesty, virtuous.
14	Pure love, devotion.	33	Admirable, worthy, honorable.
15	Beauty, adoration.	34	Endurance, tolerance, discomfort.
16	Love, sexuality, honesty.	35	Strength, vitality, good health.
17	Inconstancy, flirtatiousness.		
18	Obstinacy, narrow-mindedness.		
19	No reading.		

36 Inspirational, motivational, adept.

37 Goodness, tolerance, physical love.

38 Greed, faults, desire.

39 No reading.

40 Conviviality, joyfulness, fun.

41 Misdeeds, offense, lacking merit.

42 Travel, risk, sorrow.

43 Pious, righteous, spiritual.

44 Pride, pageantry, capability.

45 Imagination, thought, fruitfulness.

46 Abundance, affluence, rural.

47 Fortunate, longevity, health.

48 Verdict, sentence, disappointment.

49 No reading.

50 Freedom after confinement.

60 Loss, loneliness, solitude.

70 Rational, logical, scientific.

80 Longevity, restoration, health.

90 Undiscerning, lacking discrimination.

100 Success, reward, glory.

200 Hesitation, indecision, weakness.

300 Serene, calm, stoical.

400 Beauty, culture, over-reaction.

500 Reward, acceptance, honor.

600 Enmity, ill will, suspicion.

700 Moral fiber, strength, vitality.

800 Power, glory, travel.

900 Reward, power, modesty.

1000 Ultimate success.

Let's assume we are analyzing the qualities of someone called Bernard Seymour. First we work out the numerological value of the name, using the letter-number correspondences on the Hand of Fatima (page 60).

B	2		S	90
E	5		E	5
R	80		Y	400
N	40		M	30
A	1		O	50
R	80		U	200
D	4		R	80

This gives us a total of 1,067. For purposes of interpretation, this number is split to create 1,000, 60, and 7. This means that Bernard will achieve ultimate success (1,000), after experiencing loss, loneliness, and solitude (60). He will spend a great deal of time thinking and contemplating, and will retain a sense of innocence (7).

Here is another example, which shows what happens when the total exceeds 1,999. His name is Xavier van Zutov.

X	300		V	700
A	1		A	1
V	700		N	40
I	9		Z	500
E	5		U	200
R	80		T	100
			O	50
			V	700

This totals 3,386. Because the interpretation numbers do not go beyond a possible 1,999, we eliminate two of the thousands in Xavier's name, which gives us a new total of 1,386. This is then broken down to 1,000, 300, 80, and 6. This tells us that Xavier will ultimately be extremely successful (1,000), helped by his peaceful, calm, and stoical nature (300). He will lead a long life, blessed with good health (80), and will achieve a great deal of satisfaction through his work and career (6).

4

lucky charms

EVERYONE WANTS TO be lucky. Throughout history, people have carried lucky charms with them in the hopes that it will make them more attractive, more intelligent, and bring them more wealth and good fortune.

Primitive people believed that every misfortune was caused by malevolent spirits. Fortunately, though, every community had a shaman, sorcerer, magician, medicine man, or priest who was able to neutralize the evil spirits by reciting or singing chants or songs.

Spoken charms were still being recited in medieval times. A charm that allegedly cured a bleeding nose was to make the sign of the cross three times, and then say the Lord's Prayer three times. After that, the sufferer had to say an Ave Maria, and then repeat the words "Max, Hackx," "Lyacx," "Iseus," and "Christus."

A less complicated spoken charm was used to help sufferers of epilepsy. You had to hold the afflicted person by his or her hand and whisper into his or her ear, "I conjure thee by the sun and moon, and by the Gospel of the day delivered by God to Hubert, Giles, Cornelius and John, that thou rise and fall no more."[1]

Francis Barrett, the nineteenth-century cabalist and author, strongly believed in the power of words and claimed to have caused "terrible rains and claps of thunder" by saying certain words. He wrote, "Almost all charms are impotent without words, because words are the speech of the speaker, and the image of the thing signified or spoken of; therefore, whatever wonderful effect is intended, let the same be performed with the addition of words significative of the will or desire of the operator." Barrett included a charm for his readers intended to stop a "flux of blood." He was so certain of the success of this charm that he wrote, "I dare lay down my life for the success, and entire cure." The person saying the words has to hold the patient's hand, and say, "In the blood of Adam arose death—in the blood of Christ death is extinguished—in the same blood of Christ I command thee, O, blood, that thou stop fluxing!"[2]

Gradually, people realized that a spoken or sung charm was essentially ephemeral. A solid object was permanent, and consequently, small objects, especially objects that had enjoyed contact with something special, became known as charms. An object that had been held or owned by a saint, for instance, would make a highly effective charm. The term "touch wood" relates to this. When people touched a splinter of wood that they believed came from the cross of Jesus, they felt lucky and blessed.

Charms are intended to bring good luck. A person's wealth or status have no bearing on this. Even John D. Rockefeller carried a lucky stone with him everywhere he went.[3]

A Catalog of Charms

Almost anything you care to imagine has been worn or carried as good luck charm at one time or another. What follows are some of the better known ones. Many of these charms have also served as amulets or talismans at various times in history.

ACORN

An acorn charm symbolizes vigor, power, and energy. It can help you achieve your long-term goals by making the path ahead smoother than would otherwise be the case. (See also page 31.)

ANKH

The ankh is an ancient Egyptian object that symbolizes life in all its forms, particularly everlasting life. In fact, it is sometimes referred to as the cross of life. It is formed from a T-shaped cross with an oval loop at the top. Pharaohs were often depicted holding an ankh.

It is a charm that symbolizes life and prevents illness and disease. (See also page 32.)

BADGER'S TOOTH

Gamblers once sewed a badger's tooth inside the right-hand pocket of their waistcoats to provide them with luck at cards.

BEE

Wearing a bee charm is believed to be a sign of good luck. If a bee comes indoors and is reluctant to leave, it is considered a sign that a visitor is on his or her way. It is also a sign of good luck if a bee flies into your home and then leaves. However, it is considered bad luck when a bee dies inside your house.

At one time bees were believed to be messengers of the gods. The so-called "wisdom of the bees" is probably connected with this.

BIRD

Wearing a bird charm is believed to fill the wearer with zest and energy for life. He or she will derive happiness from every moment of the day.

Traditionally, birds were believed to be able to speak with humans. In the Bible we read, "Curse not the king, no not in thy thought; and curse not the rich in thy bed-chamber: for a bird of the air shall carry the voice, and that which hath wings shall tell the matter" (Ecclesiastes 10:20). The well-known expression "A little bird told me" probably came from this.

BUTTERFLY

Butterfly charms signify good health and happiness. Butterflies symbolize summer with all its freedoms and joys. Wearing a butterfly charm shows that you have a sense of playfulness and fun. In the East, butterfly ornaments and charms indicate a desire for a long and happy life. Traditionally, it was considered a good sign if a white butterfly settled near you. A yellow butterfly, on the other hand, indicated an illness.

BUTTON

A shiny button is believed to attract new friends. It is considered a sign of life-long friendship if someone gives you a button. The best button to use as a lucky charm is one that you find, but any button will work. My grandmother had a large collection of buttons, which she kept in a metal tin. She would shake the buttons inside the tin whenever she felt the need for luck. (See also page 32.)

CAT

Cats have had an interesting history, being both revered and hated at different times. The ancient Egyptians considered the cat sacred, and it was a capital offense to kill one. In Norse mythology, Freya, the goddess of marriage, rode in a carriage pulled by cats. In an attempt to eradicate pagan beliefs, the Christians called Freya a witch. Naturally, the cats who accompanied her were also condemned, and people came to believe that they worked for the powers of darkness. This is why, even today, the popular impression of a witch is that of an old woman accompanied by her familiar, a black cat. Fortunately, the reputation of cats gradually improved. Soldiers returning from the Crusades accidentally brought black rats with them, and the plague that the rats introduced ravaged Europe. Suddenly, cats were needed again.

Because of their incredible sensitivity, aloofness, and love of the night, cats have always been considered psychic.[4] It is believed that they can sense invisible energies that people cannot detect. Consequently, a cat charm promotes these special qualities. A multicolored cat charm is believed to attract an abundance of good luck.

In Japan, the Meneki-neko cat is a famous charm that is used by shop owners to attract money. Meneki-neko is porcelain cat, who sits with one paw raised in the air as if it were waving. In actuality, the cat is beckoning in wealth. You have probably seen examples of these in Chinese restaurants and other places that sell Asian products.

COIN

A popular one-liner says that a lucky coin is any coin that happens to be in your possession. In fact, a lucky coin is any coin that you find, and the best coin of all to find is one minted in the year of your birth. You can turn it into a pendant or simply keep it in your pocket or purse. However you carry it, it will attract good fortune to you. Other dates are considered propitious for coins. If the date on the coin is that of a leap year, for instance, it is believed to be twice as lucky. Keep these coins in the kitchen, and they will provide unexpected good luck. Take good care of your lucky coin, though, as it is believed that your luck will take a turn for the worse if you lose it.

Coins have been known to be lucky for more than just individuals, as this example shows. Singapore is one of my favorite countries, and I visit it regularly. I first learned about feng shui in Singapore, back in the late 1960s. Because of my interest in feng shui, I was not at all surprised when Singapore issued an octagonal dollar coin. This shape, known as a *pa-kua*, shows the four cardinal directions, plus the four intermediary ones. It is important in feng shui, as the eight trigrams of the I Ching are placed around this octagonal symbol. This pa-kua is one of the most important remedies in feng shui, as it is believed to avert or ward off negative influences. Consequently, the eight-sided octagon is considered a lucky symbol, and an eight-sided coin is naturally considered a lucky charm.

The dollar coin was introduced in the 1980s when the Singapore economy was in decline because of the building of their mass transit railway system. A popular story in Singapore, which may or may not be true, is that the then prime minister, Lee Kuan Yew, was advised by a feng shui expert to introduce the coin to avert the negative effects caused by the tunneling of the railway. The economy was supposed to improve if everyone in the country had a pa-kua. The only way to do that was to issue the octagonal dollar coin. Unfortunately, this did not solve the problem, as the octagon was kept in people's pockets and purses, rather than in open view. (The eventual solution was to change the shape of the road tax labels from round to octagonal. Everyone displays these in their cars, and the economy started booming again.) One additional side benefit of the octagonal dollar coin is that thousands of tourists take them home as a souvenir of their visit (at this moment, I have one beside me as I write). The pa-kua coin is definitely a lucky coin for Singapore.

CORNUCOPIA

The cornucopia, or horn of plenty, is an ancient charm that brings good luck and abundance to anyone who wears it. It is believed that wearers of these will always have enough of everything. Whatever he or she needs will become available when required.

Cornucopias are generally made of silver or gold and are worn around the neck on a chain. Horn-shaped seashells are also sometimes used as cornucopias.

DAISIES & DANDELIONS

The humble daisy is related to love and romance. This is why people still pick a daisy and remove the petals one by one, while reciting, "She loves me, she loves me not," until the last petal is reached. I remember doing this with dandelions, rather than daisies. We would blow the dandelion until the entire cottony top was gone. Each breath was related to "She loves me, she loves me not." Another version of this was to close your eyes, make a wish, and then blow vigorously at the dandelion. If the entire top came off with one blow, the wish would be granted.

Wearing a daisy or dandelion charm is believed to attract the right partner to you.

DOG

Dogs have been considered man's best friend for some twenty-thousand years. Their friendly, loving, and forgiving natures make them arguably our most loved pet. These qualities are also transmuted into a dog charm or pendant. Wearing a dog charm means that you will feel protected at all times.

DOVE

The dove has always been considered a symbol of purity, and wearing a dove charm means that you are surrounding yourself with a purity that others will sense and respect.

EAR

A charm in the form of an ear is considered extremely lucky. Others will be keen to hear what you have to say, and you will be able to listen better than ever before. Make sure that the charm is of a right ear, though, as that means that nothing but good will be heard or said about you.

EYE

A charm in the form of a right eye will bring increased happiness to you and will also benefit your friends. (See also page 15.)

FAN

A fan-shaped charm is believed to grant the wearer confidence and authority. It also provides protection. The fan's history shows how it came to symbolize confidence and authority. In ancient Egypt, servants stood behind important guests and fanned them with large papyrus fans. As only rich and important people were able to employ servants to operate fans, the fan came to indicate prestige and wealth, and this naturally provides confidence and authority

FISH

The fish is a symbol of the Christian church, but is by no means exclusive to it. This possibly came about because the Greek word for "fish," *ikhthus* (also often spelled ichthys in English), creates an acronym of the initial letters of "Jesus Christ, Son of God, Saviour" in Greek. It also may have derived from the feeding of the five thousand told in the Bible (John 6:9), or possibly from the fact that several of Jesus' disciples were fishermen.

A fish charm attracts wealth, abundance, and increase.

FOUR-LEAF CLOVER

If you asked someone to name a lucky charm, he or she will probably say, "Four-leaf clover." This ancient Irish charm has traditionally been used to attract good luck, and it would be hard to find someone who hasn't looked for one. It is believed that you will enjoy good fortune for a whole year if you pick a four leafed clover in May.

Each leaf represents a different aspect of life, aspects which are covered in the old rhyme:

> One leaf is for fame,
> And one leaf is for wealth,
> And one is for a faithful lover,
> And one to bring you glorious health,
> Are all in the four-leaved clover.

A charming ancient legend says that Eve took a four-leaf clover with her when she was banished from the Garden of Eden.

Wearing a four-leaf clover as a charm is believed to eliminate unpleasant surprises.

FROG AND TOAD

Frogs and toads, along with cats, were considered to be familiars of witches. There is an old legend that says that toads carried gemstones in the knob on their skulls between and slightly above their eyes. Shakespeare mentions this in *As You Like It* (II, i).

> Sweet are the uses of adversity,
> Which like the toad, ugly and venomous,
> Wears yet a precious jewel in its head.

In the past, unethical people sold "toadstones," made from fused borax and other substances, as amulets, which they claimed came from living toads, who readily discharged their stones when placed on a scarlet cloth.

People have always regarded frogs and toads with a mixture of fascination and fear. Their clammy skins and ability to live in two environments at the same time were a factor in this. However, the major factor, was their cold, jewel-like, staring eyes that intimidated people. Not surprisingly, people have long credited toads and frogs with strange, supernatural powers.

In the past, some people believed that frogs contained the souls of dead children.[5] However, in ancient Egypt, frogs were considered so important that they were embalmed after death. In the first century C.E., Pliny the Elder concluded that frog charms attracted friends and everlasting love. Ever since then, frogs and toads have been popular charms.

HAND

Hands have always been considered lucky. For maximum benefit the palm of the hand should be clearly visible on a charm in the shape of a hand. The palm stops any evil from reaching you by pushing it away. A hand charm also allows you to receive what is rightfully yours.

A hand with the first and second fingers extended, but with the thumb, third and fourth fingers closed, is a sign of a blessing. In some parts of the world, a hand with just the first finger outstretched is considered protection against the evil eye (see page 22).[6]

Strangely enough, the severed hands of dead people were at one time considered lucky. Thieves used to touch the hand of a dead thief, believing that it would grant them good fortune. The right hand of Father Edmund Arrowsmith, a Catholic priest executed in England in 1628, is preserved in the church of St. Oswald in Ashton, England, and attracts pilgrims to this day. The pilgrims touch the hand, believing that it can cure a variety of diseases and afflictions.[7]

HEART

The heart has been considered the seat of the soul since Egyptian times. Once the soul left the heart, the body would die. Many faiths believe that hearts will be weighed at the day of judgment, and only people with perfect hearts will be allowed to proceed into the afterlife. Today, the heart is considered a token of pure love, and when two lovers exchange this charm it signifies that they are giving each other their hearts.

HOLLY

Holly is closely connected with marriage. Consequently, wearing a holly charm is believed to help you attract the right partner. Wearing it after you are married ensures that the relationship will be a happy one. It is also believed that you should place a holly charm under your pillow whenever you are experiencing marital problems. If you do this, you will experience pleasant dreams that will help you resolve the problem.

Holly was considered a symbol of friendship in ancient Rome, and people would send it to each other as a gift. Holly gradually became associated with love, and then ultimately marriage. Along the way, Christians adopted it, as its prickly leaves reminded them of the crown of thorns that Jesus wore, and the red berries symbolized the blood that Jesus shed.

HORSE

Horse charms vary in their meaning depending on their color. A white horse attracts good luck, while a black horse invites mystery. Neither is considered to be better than the other.

Horse charms symbolize strength and courage. In the East, horses' hooves were used as charms in people's homes, as they symbolized a high status. This is because someone who rode in a horse-drawn chariot was obviously important.[8] The horse is also one of the twelve signs of the Chinese horoscope, and symbolizes happiness and a successful career.

HORSESHOE

Horseshoes are classic lucky charms. Although you can buy a horseshoe, it is much better to find one. Traditionally, a horseshoe should hang above the front door to ensure that the good luck stays inside the house. The crescent shape of a horseshoe has been considered protective. It was also believed to deter witches and the devil—perhaps because horseshoes are nailed with seven nails, and seven has always been considered a spiritual number. (Even the iron nails used to fasten horseshoes are considered to be charms or amulets, see page 12.)

The way you hang a lucky horseshoe is a matter of some importance. I always thought that blacksmiths were the only people who could hang horseshoes with the points facing downward and that everyone else had to hang them pointing upwards. This allowed you to contain the good luck inside the arms of the horseshoe, while the fortunate blacksmith could allow the good luck to flow freely into his premises. However, I now find there are two schools of thought on which way the horseshoe should be attached to the house. If the horseshoe points upwards, the luck is believed to be contained within the bowl-like shape. This shape is also believed to suck the devil inside, and prevent him from entering the house. If you hang it downward, the horseshoe becomes a magnet that attracts good luck. However, people who prefer the horseshoe pointing upwards say that downward pointing horseshoes allow the luck to run out. The opposing point of view is that a downward pointing horseshoe allows a continuous flow of good luck to rain upon the occupants. Whichever way you decide to hang it, the luckiest horseshoe is one that you find by chance. These are believed to contain much more luck than a shoe that is purchased.

LADYBUG OR LADYBIRD

Ladybug brooches and badges make attractive orna-ments and are also worn as lucky charms to attract good luck and prosperity. It is considered bad luck to kill a la-dybug. The ladybug has always had sacred associations, and this is apparent from the different names the insect has in different countries.

There is a tradition that links the ladybug with the Virgin Mary. In the Middle Ages, the ladybird received her current name. At this time, the beetle was dedicated to the Virgin Mary and was known as "beetle of our Lady."[9]

The origins of this old nursery rhyme are unknown, and it first appeared in printed form in about 1744.

Ladybird, ladybird,
 Fly away home,
Your house is on fire
 And your children all gone;
All except one
 And that's little Ann
And she has crept under
 The warming pan.

The rhyme has been interpreted in a number of ways. In Germany it is believed that the rhyme was originally a charm to help the sun pass through sunset. The house on fire symbolized the red evening sky. The Rosicrucians believe that the rhyme has links with Isis, an Egyptian deity, and they also relate it to the Egyptian scarab.[10] The most likely explanation for the traditional rhyme is the traditional burning of the hop vines after harvest. This cleared the fields, but killed many ladybugs in the process.

LEAVES

Leaves have always been used as lucky charms by people living in the country. The four-leaf clover is an obvious example, but there are many others. A shamrock leaf was supposed to ensure good fortune. Wishing caps, made from hazel leaves and twigs, were worn in many European countries. It was believed that if you wore them, your wish would be granted. Wearing a wreath of rosemary was believed to improve your memory. People also believed that they could overcome obstacles if they carried a sprig of springwort around with them.

A charm showing a number of leaves is believed to protect you from minor ailments, especially in winter. This is because leaves symbolize vigor and good health.

LIZARD

The lizard is usually found on finger rings, though it can also be worn as a brooch or pendant. In Portugal, porcelain lizards are attached to the walls of houses to attract good luck. The lizard is usually worn as a charm to enhance the wearer's eyesight. This is because the emerald green color of the lizard symbolizes the emerald gem, which has always been believed to enhance vision.

MANDRAKE

Mandrake is the root of the mandragora plant. It is shaped like a turnip, and is often forked, giving the appearance of two legs, which makes it look like a man. It has been used as an aphrodisiac and narcotic for thousands of years. It is referred to as an aphrodisiac in the Bible in Genesis (30:14) and in this verse from the Song of Solomon (7:13).

> Come, my beloved, let us go forth into the fields, and lodge in the villages;
> let us go out early to the vineyards, and see whether the vines have budded, whether the grape blossoms have opened and the pomegranates are in bloom. There I will give you my love.
> The mandrakes give forth fragrance, and over our doors are all choice fruits, new as well as old, which I have laid up for you, O my beloved.

It became a charm in the Middle Ages when it was believed that the mandrake could provide wealth, happiness, and fertility. Whole roots were sometimes carried on a cord around the person's neck, but more commonly, small figures were made from the roots and worn as charms.[11]

MISTLETOE

When someone stands under the mistletoe, he or she expects a kiss. The custom of kissing under the mistletoe comes from Scandinavia, where enemies who wished to become reconciled would meet under the mistletoe and exchange a kiss of peace.[12] There is a Viking legend that tells how Friga, the Norse goddess of love, cried when her son, Baldur, was restored to life. Friga's tears turned into white mistletoe berries. Today, anyone who kisses under mistletoe is believed to receive Friga's personal protection. It did not take long for people to realize that any two people could kiss under the mistletoe, and a happy tradition began. Consequently, a mistletoe charm is used to attract love and romance.

MONEY SWORD

The traditional Chinese money sword, made of coins and red thread, has become a popular charm again, thanks to the increasing interest around the world in feng shui. Money swords were traditionally hung over the head of the bed, though they can be displayed anywhere. It is a charm to attract prosperity and good luck.

OWL

The owl is a charm to enhance wisdom, knowledge, and common sense. The expression "wise as an owl" derives from this. Owls were common in Athens, and Athene was symbolized by the owl. In Rome, it was considered a bad omen to see an owl in the daytime. This is because owls are nocturnal and should not be seen in daylight hours.

Owl charms have traditionally been worn to provide commonsense and wisdom. However, some people believe that your financial position will improve if you carry an owl charm in, or close to, your wallet or purse.[13]

PEARL

Pearls have been valued and revered for thousands of years. In ancient Rome they were so valued that a law was passed forbidding people below a certain rank from wearing them.[14] Pearls hung from the branches of the mystical Hindu Kalpa Tree, and a pearl is also one of the nine jewels in the Nav-Ratna, the most famous and revered of all Hindu talismans. In Islam, six of the Seven Heavens were made of precious objects, including pearls.[15]

A single pearl carried in your pocket or purse makes a charm that helps restore your physical body and grants you peace of mind. Pearls provide love, respect, kindness, and sympathy. People who wear or carry them are believed to lead smooth, harmonious lives.

PENTAGRAM

The pentagram—also known as a pentacle or wizard's foot—is a five-pointed star. It has been used as an amulet to protect the wearer from evil influences. It is also believed to symbolize the five senses, and, because it can be split into three triangles, it is sometimes used to represent the Holy Trinity. It can also be used to symbolize a person, with its points representing a head, two arms, and two legs. Leonardo da Vinci's "Vitruvian Man," his famous drawing depicting the proportions of man, is a good example. It consists of a circle, inside which is a naked man with his arms and legs outstretched. The circle is a feminine symbol of protection, creating a picture of male and female harmony.

Traditionally, it is believed that when the single point faces upwards the pentagram is a symbol of good (white magic), but when the single point heads downward, it is a symbol of evil (black magic). The pentacle is often used in ceremonial magic, as it effectively blocks evil spirits. It is a charm against evil.

PHOENIX

The Greek legend of the fabulous phoenix is well-known. According to legend, this bird, after living for hundreds of years, makes a nest of spices, and then sets fire to it by flapping its wings. The bird burns to ashes but then returns to life again. Several alchemists used the phoenix as their symbol, and it has also been used to symbolize the resurrection. As a charm, it is used to symbolize renewal, new starts, and a new life.

RABBIT'S FOOT

The rabbit's foot is a charm that symbolizes fruitfulness and good luck. The good luck element comes from the belief that rabbits are born with their eyes open, and this gives them power over the evil eye (see chapter 2).[16] The hind legs of a rabbit touch the ground before the front legs. Thousands of years ago, people considered this so unusual that they credited the back feet with magical powers.

A rabbit's foot charm should always be kept in the left pocket. Traditionally, the best rabbit's foot charm is one that contains the left hind foot of an animal that has been killed by a cross-eyed person at full moon.

The great physicist Niels Bohr was asked why he had a rabbit's foot attached to his laboratory door. "I'm told that it brings luck whether one believes in it or not," he replied.[17]

ROSE

A red rose charm symbolizes faithfulness in love. As long as you are being true to your partner, this charm will protect you. A white rose charm symbolizes purity in thought, word, and deed.

SCARAB

The scarab is possibly the best-known Egyptian charm. Hundreds of thousands of them were made over a two-thousand-year period.[18] The scarab, or dung beetle, uses its back legs to roll balls of dung to its underground home for food. Because it cannot see where it is going, it often takes a circuitous route over numerous obstacles. The dung beetle's hard work reminded the ancient Egyptians of the sun's daily journey across the sky. The eggs inside the dung eventually hatch, symbolizing creation.

The scarab is worn as a charm for good health and virility. It also signifies resurrection, regeneration, and birth.

SHIP

The ship is an early Christian charm used to protect the wearer when traveling across water. It originally signified a ship carrying believers across the sea of life to the Promised Land. Consequently, it was also worn to protect the wearer from the temptations of the flesh, to ensure that they were saved.

SAINT CHRISTOPHER'S MEDAL

This well-known charm protects travelers. St. Christopher, the patron saint of all travelers, was a third-century Christian martyr. Legend has it that Christopher lived near a river and often helped travelers make the crossing. One day, he carried a child over the river. The child became more and more heavy, and St. Christopher barely made it to the other side. When he commented to the child on this, the child told him that he had just borne all the world and its sins on his shoulders. The river was the River of Death, and the child he carried was Christ. His name is derived from the Latin word *christophorus*, which means "one who carries Christ." The St. Christopher's medal shows the saint carrying the child.

SNAKE

Wearing a snake charm is believed to protect you against your enemies. It is also believed to provide the wearer with longevity, intelligence, and insight. At one time it was considered evil, because of the serpent in the Garden of Eden. However, people came to realize that the misfortunes of Adam and Eve were of their own making and could not be blamed on the serpent.

SPIDER

It has always been a fortunate sign to see a spider. For instance, in England, it was thought that money was coming your way if a spider landed on your clothing. Conversely, it is considered bad luck to kill a spider.

Wearing a spider charm is believed to protect you from unexpected problems. It also bestows shrewdness and financial acumen on people who wear it.

SWASTIKA

It may seem surprising to find the swastika listed as a good luck charm. However, until the days of Nazi Germany, the swastika was used to attract good luck, happiness, and longevity. The directions indicated by the swastika can represent the four cardinal directions, the four seasons, and even the four winds. In prehistoric times, the swastika was used all around the world, including by the pre-Columbian Native Americans, Hindus, Chinese, British, and Etruscans. The early Christians used it as a secret emblem in Roman times.[19]

Swastika comes from the Sanskrit *su*, meaning "well," and *asti*, which means "being."

TORTOISE AND TURTLE

In the East, the tortoise symbolizes longevity. Tortoise amulets dating back to the Neolithic period have been found in Egypt, making them among the oldest of all magical objects.[20]

When worn as a charm, the tortoise gives patience, stability, and longevity.

WISHBONE

The furcula, better known as the wishbone, from a chicken or turkey makes a highly effective charm that gathers good fortune for you. Naturally, both people have to make a wish when the wishbone is pulled. The person who receives the capped end will have his or her wish granted, but the other person will also receive a pleasant surprise in the near future. You can simply carry an intact wishbone with you as a lucky charm, if you don't have someone to pull it with. (There is no need to keep the broken pieces of the wishbone after it has been pulled.)

chapter 4

Finding Lucky Charms

Almost anything can be used as a lucky charm. A treasured object that someone has given you makes an extremely powerful good luck charm because of the personal associations it provides. Most charms are purchased ready-made, but you can make your own, if you wish. As with talismans, making lucky charms yourself provides a great deal of additional power and energy.

Museum stores and jewelry shops are both good places to browse for suitable charms, but you will find them everywhere once you become aware of them.

Charm bracelets are still popular and allow the owner to wear many different charms at the same time. Just recently, I attended a christening at which the baby was presented with a charm bracelet full of miniature silver charms. Although the baby was only a couple of months old, she already had a collection of charms!

Charms can be worn or simply carried with you in some convenient way. They do not need to be visible to be effective. Consequently, you can attach a charm to an undergarment or carry it in your purse or wallet, if you do not want other people to see it.

making & charging talismans

LUCKY CHARMS AND amulets can usually be found or bought, but talismans almost always have to be made. This is because they are intended for a particular purpose, and the user's mind, body, and emotions are all involved in the process of creating the talisman. When you make your own talisman you are joining the ranks of many famous magicians, such as Cornelius Agrippa, Albertus Magnus, Theophrastus, Paracelsus, and Peter d'Abano. These pioneers considered talismans to be one of the best ways to contact spiritual forces and to compel them to conform to the will of the magician. It is important to remember that talismans are not lucky charms or simple decorations, but important magical tools that are dedicated to you and your goals.

Focusing the Power of Your Mind

You need to remain focused on your goal the whole time you are working on your talisman. Your will power and intent play a vital role in creating an effective talisman. Your belief in the power of what you are doing is also essential. If you doubt the power of your mind, there is a simple experiment you can do to banish those doubts.

Pour two glasses of water from the same source. Hold one of the glasses and silently bless the water in the glass. Think pleasant thoughts about the water for at least thirty seconds. Put that glass down, and then pick up the second glass. This time think negative thoughts about the water you are holding. Tell it how much you hate and despise it. Do this for at least thirty seconds. After doing this, take a sip from each glass. Even though the water came from the same source, the blessed water will taste much better than the water that was cursed. An alternative way of doing this experiment is to ask someone to mix the glasses up while you are not looking. You should find it easy to determine which glass was which.

Water can be affected by your thoughts, and so can any of the materials that are used in making talismans: paper, parchment, wood, and metal. By thinking of your ultimate purpose while working on the talisman, you will imbue the object with the vital energy that is required to make it effective. In every aspect of your life, what you think and feel manifests itself and becomes a reality. This is especially the case when strong emotions are involved. This is simply the law of cause and effect.

Making a talisman allows this law to work for your own benefit.

Naturally, you cannot rely upon the talisman to do all the work for you in making your desires a reality. You will still have to work at whatever it is you want. The talisman will aid and help you in the task, by influencing your subconscious mind.

Some people think that the talisman itself has some strange magic power. This is not the case. When you make and consecrate a talisman you are charging it with a powerful magnetic energy that flows through the talisman and on to you. The power is in you, rather than in the parchment or metal that comprises the talisman. The talisman is a tool that needs to be used wisely and responsibly.

The Elements of a Talisman

Four fundamental elements are essential to the success of any talisman.

MATERIAL

Careful thought should be given to the material that you choose to use. The appearance of the finished talisman plays a role in its final effectiveness. A beautifully engraved circle of silver looks much more magical and powerful than the same design scrawled on a piece of paper torn from a notebook. It pays to use the best materials that you can find when making a talisman.

The materials used to form a talisman are an important part of the finished object. Talismans are usually made of parchment, vellum, or metal. Traditionally, gold was the metal of choice, but nowadays most magicians use copper. Copper makes a good substitute for gold, as it is relatively inexpensive and, because it is soft, is easy to engrave. Other metals are also used, depending on the planetary correspondences for the particular talisman (see appendix A).

Traditional talismans tend to look magical because they are usually inscribed in Hebrew or Latin or a magical alphabet (see appendix E) and contain a great deal of symbolism that relates to their specific purpose. Consequently, many talismans are made from a material that is easy to write and draw on. Paper can be used, but it makes a poor substitute for better materials and should only be used for a temporary talisman. Good-quality paper should be used, even for temporary talismans.

Parchment, which comes from sheep and goat hides specially prepared to make them suitable for writing, is another option. Vellum, which is made from calfskin, is the best but also the most expensive option. Talismans can also be made from glass, leather, bone, or any other material that you find aesthetically pleasing.

Whatever the material, it should be virgin, which means it has not previously been used for any other purpose. Many years ago, I became interested in papermaking, mainly because it enabled me to create my own parchment-like paper. I made the interesting discovery that talismans made from recycled paper did not seem to have as much power and energy as talismans made from paper that came from virgin sources, such as plants.

Even more important than appearance is the fact that everything in the universe vibrates at a certain frequency. Consequently, when choosing suitable materials, hold a variety of alternatives in your hands and see which one feels right for you. Different materials will feel right for you at different times, depending on the type of talisman you are constructing.

DESIGN

There is no limit to what you can inscribe on your talisman. Traditionally, magic squares, sigils, astrological symbols, and sacred characters have all been used (and we'll discuss these and more in subsequent chapters). However, you can write anything at all that seems right for you at the time. A short poem or prayer might be what you require, and you might choose to write it in a magical alphabet (see appendix E) or perhaps Hebrew or Latin. It is often a good idea to use both words and symbols, as they affect different hemispheres in the brain.

Remember that whatever you place on your talisman is what is required at the time you make it and will work for you. No special artistic gifts are required. Also remember that, though the specific designs and words are of vital importance, they have no real power until the talisman is charged. This transforms the talisman into a vibrant, powerful source of energy that works like a magnet, attracting to it the desires and aims of its owner. We'll get to charging talismans soon.

ENERGY

While making and consecrating your talisman you need to remain clearly focused on your purpose for making it. Your personal energy and intent is vital to the success of the talisman. You might choose a certain time in the day or a specific day of the week during which to work on your talisman, as this adds universal energies to your own. The combination of personal and universal energies creates spiritual power, making the talisman even more effective.

BELIEF

There is no point in making a talisman unless you believe that it will work for you. Our beliefs always manifest themselves in our lives. If you believe in your heart that you will always be poor, for instance, you will develop a poverty consciousness that ensures that your belief becomes a reality, and you will remain poor. Belief in your talisman becomes reinforced every time you see or touch it. It affects your subconscious mind, which then attracts to you whatever you believe.

Making a Talisman

THE CONDITIONS

To make an effective talisman, you'll need the proper conditions. For some talismans, certain astrological elements need to be in place in addition to these general guidelines.

Time

Decide on the right time to make your talisman. You may have no choice in this matter and may have to work on it at any time when you will not be interrupted. If you can, though, work on it during the appropriate planetary hours (as described beginning on page 47 in chapter 3) or use the following times as a guide.

- Sunday: 11:00 AM to 1:00 PM
- Monday: 6:00 PM to 6:00 AM Tuesday
- Tuesday: 11:00 AM to 1:00 PM
- Wednesday: 6:00 AM to 8:00 AM
- Thursday: 1:00 PM to 5:00 PM
- Friday: 6:00 AM to 8:00 AM
- Saturday: 3:00 PM to 5:00 PM

Place

Choose a quiet place where you will not be interrupted. Make sure that you have everything you require ahead of time, so that you will not need to stop while you are working on your talisman.

Mood

Start with a few moments of silence. Many people offer a prayer at this point, asking for divine guidance and protection. You might say something along these lines: "Almighty God, please help and guide me as I prepare this talisman for [whatever purpose you have in mind]. I have the right motives for doing this and hope and pray it will benefit everyone concerned. Please bless this talisman and everyone who is affected by it. Thank you for your help and protection. Amen."

Naturally, you can pray to any deity you choose. Most people I know send a prayer to their guardian angel, but this is not essential. You might send a message to the Creator of the Universe or the Creative Life Force, if you have no particular deity in mind. You may choose to stand in silence until you can feel the universal energies surrounding you.

WORKING ON THE OBJECT

These guidelines apply to any talisman you might choose to make, whether it be a magic square from chapter 7 or one of the traditional talismans or something entirely of your own design. You might want to start, though, with the astrological talisman outlined on page 100.

When you feel ready, you can start work on the object that will become your talisman. Think about your aims in making it, and visualize the benefits that will accrue once you have the completed talisman in your possession. Keep focused on these benefits the whole time you are working on your talisman.

Do not concern yourself with perfection. If you have little or no artistic ability, your talisman may look rough and ready. That does not matter. You are making a magical tool that will help you, not a work of art. Remember that we all do the very best we are capable of at any given moment. The talisman you construct will be the very best that you can do at that particular time.

If possible, start and finish your talisman in the same session. If you have to stop for any reason while working on it, offer another prayer asking for protection for both you and the unfinished talisman while you are away.

You will intuitively know when to stop. I know people who make extremely elaborate talismans and find it difficult to put their tools down as they want to continually add to the design. However, even these people finally realize that they have done all they need to do.

Once it is made, the talisman can be stored in a pouch made of silk to protect it from harm. Silk is used because it keeps the energies inside. It is not a good conductor of spiritual power. The talisman should be stored in a safe place or carried with you.

Once the talisman is complete, it needs to be charged before it can work. Your concentration and focus while making the talisman mean that it is partially charged anyway, but the process of charging it is still necessary, as it gives it even more power and energy. When you charge your talisman you are giving it the necessary power to manifest your will. We'll get to charging in a few pages.

MAKING AN ASTROLOGICAL TALISMAN

We can now use what we have learned thus far to create an astrological talisman for a specific goal. For the purposes of this example, we'll say that you are a Gemini and you want to receive more recognition for the work you do.

You could start by inscribing a two- to three-inch-diameter circle on parchment or a sheet of good quality paper. Consult the table on page 195 of appendix A to see the various correspondences for Gemini (we see from the table that the element for Gemini is quicksilver so you could also create the talisman out of silver, if you prefer). In the center of the circle, place something to represent your sign. You might draw two people to represent the twins, or you might use the glyph that symbolizes Gemini. If you wish, you could draw this in yellow, as yellow is the color that relates to Gemini. Alternatively, you might choose to use yellow for the background of the circle. As Mercury is the planet that relates to Gemini, you might choose to draw a winged messenger above or below the symbol for Gemini.

Now you need to think about the reason why you are constructing the talisman. Your main aim is to receive more recognition. Consult the tables in appendix A. This is a tenth house matter. Consequently, you might choose to draw a small goat (to symbolize Capricorn, who rules the tenth house) to the right- or left-hand side of your Gemini symbol. You could draw this using black or brown, as these are the colors of Capricorn. Recognition is often related to money (second house) and career (sixth house) because they are all earth houses. If these factors apply in your case, the symbols that represent them (bull and virgin) should be added to your talisman, again using the correct colors. If the recognition is related to your relationships with others, you might add a water bearer to symbolize the eleventh house.

Each of the planets is aided by an angel and you might write the name of the relevant angel (listed on the table) around the circumference of your talisman. Any person seeking recognition would inscribe probably Cassiel (the angel that aids Capricorn) around his or her talisman.

On the reverse side of the talisman, you might choose to write something that relates to your primary goal. This might be a single word—"recognition," in this example—or you might decide to write a complete sentence, such as: "I work hard at my job, and my talisman will help me receive more recognition for the contribution I make." Some people prefer to write these messages in a magical alphabet, such as Theban (see appendix E, page 227), to keep their desires secret. Alternatively, you might draw a picture that somehow symbolizes your goal. Whenever you look at the picture, it will remind you of the talisman's purpose. (I do not allow other people to handle my talismans. Consequently, I usually write my goals down in English, as no one will see what I have written anyway.)

Another alternative is to draw a planetary magic square that relates to your goal. The person seeking more recognition would probably choose the magic square of the sun. (See chapter 7 for more on magic squares and page 163 for the sun magic square.)

THE SEVEN TRADITIONAL TALISMANS

The best known talismans are the ones relating to the seven planets. These were always made at the correct astrological times, using specific materials. There was an art in creating and consecrating these talismans. Personally, I prefer to create talismans that relate specifically to me and my needs, rather than always following traditional methods. However, magicians of the past created them in this way because they found them to be effective, and you may wish to follow in their footsteps. I have included details on how to make traditional talismans in appendix B. Be advised that the astrological parameters for consecrating these talismans are considerable. If you are not experienced with astrological calculations, you may wish to consult an astrologer to find the right day and time for making the talisman.

Charging Your Talisman

Making the physical object that will become your working talisman is only half the job. As you know, before it can work for you, a talisman must be charged. The following will show you just when and how to charge your talisman.

CONDITIONS

It is important to charge your talisman at the right time. It should not be charged while the moon is waning. The best time to charge it is shortly after the new moon. Any time while the moon is waxing is good.

Depending on the weather, you can work indoors or out. It is important that you will not be disturbed, so choose any outdoor site with care, and make sure that the temperature is warm enough. It is hard to concentrate when you are shivering with cold.

The room you charge your talisman in must be clean, tidy, and warm. You can decorate it with flowers, wall hangings, and anything else to make the room appear comforting and suitable for the task. Some people feel that you should not charge your talisman in the same room you made it in. I agree—if you are charging the talisman immediately after making it. However, you can safely use the same room as long as you allow at least one night between the making and charging stages.

Your own purity is important to charging the talisman successfully. Have a shower or bath before charging your talisman. Wear freshly washed, loosely fitted clothes, as these further emphasize purity. You can also charge your talisman in the nude, if you wish (magic users refer to this state of ritual nudity as being "skyclad"). Your talisman will benefit from being exposed to much more of your energy fields when you work naked. If you wear clothes, make sure that you wash them again after the ritual to make them suitable for everyday use again.

If desired, light a candle or two and burn incense while you charge your talisman. Any candles you use should be either white or of the right planetary color (see appendix A). Candles are powerful tools that have been used throughout magical history. Although they are frequently used as window-dressing, they are much more than that and can play a major role in successfully charging your talisman.

You might choose to have gentle background music to help you get in the right mood. Be careful not to choose any music that might prove distracting. The main benefit of music is that it obscures any sounds that may come from outside the room.

You can charge your talisman using either your own personal energy or by summoning universal energy to charge the talisman for you. The techniques are the same. However, you need to be aware of the method you prefer ahead of time so that you can visualize the necessary energies coming from you or from Mother Earth or from a divine source. A few methods for charging follow.

MANA METHOD

Mana is the vital life force, or breath of life. It is known in various cultures as ch'i, prana, or life force. It is divine spiritual energy, and we cannot survive for long without it.

The Kahunas of Hawaii believe that we consist of three parts. These parts can be regarded as different aspects of our mind, but the Kahunas visualize them as being in different parts of the body. The "high self" represents our spiritual nature and is immediately above the head. The "middle self" is the thinking side of our being and is in the brain. The "low self" is the feeling, emotional side of our natures and is found in the solar plexus. If you wish, you can relate these three selves to the superconscious, conscious, and subconscious minds.

The Kahunas believe that to achieve a goal, we first have to think about it (middle self). We then need to send it with energy to our low self, where it is charged with mana (energy) and then sent to the high self, where it will become a reality.[1]

We can use much of the Kahuna practice to charge our own talismans. To begin, stand with your feet about a foot apart. The back of your right hand should be resting on the palm of your left hand. Your talisman should be lying on your right palm, held in place by your left thumb. Close your eyes and breathe in deeply through your nose. Feel the life-sustaining mana entering your body and going deep into your lungs. Hold your breath for a few seconds before slowly exhaling. Take four or five deep breaths, until you feel that your body is full of mana. If you feel that you are not full of mana, breathe normally for thirty seconds, and then take another four or five deep breaths.

Once you have done this, sit down in a straightbacked chair and visualize yourself overflowing with mana. The Kahunas imagined themselves filled to overflowing with water, which is what they used to symbolize mana. You might choose to visualize yourself in a state of vibrant well-being. The picture you create does not matter, as long as you sense that your low self is filled to overflowing with mana energy.

Once this picture is clear in your mind, visualize a burst of energy exploding from your solar plexus and rising through your body and out of your head to form a circle of energy right above your head. The Kahunas visualize this as a gushing of water, as if a fire hose had been suddenly turned on. You might see it as a volcano of energy erupting. Again, the picture you visualize does not matter as long as you know beyond any shadow of doubt that you have sent an offering of life-enhancing, spiritual mana to your high self.

Your high self is now revitalized and ready to receive your request. Turn your right hand over, so that you are now clasping your hands with the talisman between them. Think about your need for the talisman, and superimpose an image of this need on the ball of energy above your head, in your high self. Visualize this for as long as you can. When the picture starts to fade, say your request out loud. Speak confidently, as if the talisman has already worked its magic.

The final step is to thank your high self for granting your request. Wait for several seconds before doing this. Concentrate on your breathing, and, when the time seems right, say, "Thank you, high self, for charging my talisman and for granting my request. I am grateful for all of your blessings upon me. Thank you."

Your talisman is now charged and ready for use. You will probably feel a difference in your talisman once it has been charged. Carry it with you, confident that it will be working for you every minute of the day.

DEDICATION METHOD

For this method you will need an altar. A table or shelf will do for this. However, it needs to be in a room that will not be disturbed for several hours after you have charged your talisman.

Place the talisman on the altar. Say a few words out loud to the architect of the universe, thanking him or her for protecting and guiding you.

Recite a poem that appeals to you. Naturally, this should be a serious poem that conveys thoughts that you agree with. You might choose to write your own poem especially for the occasion, but this is not essential.

Once you have finished reciting the poem, stare at the talisman for thirty seconds. After this time, speak to it, saying something like, "I empower and consecrate you for [whatever purpose you have in mind]. I imbue you with all the powers of the universe to enable you to carry out your task, and I thank you in advance for all the energy, power, and comfort that you offer to me." Stare at the talisman for another thirty seconds. Say "thank you" to the talisman, and then spread your arms out wide and look upwards, while saying "thank you" again.

Quietly leave the room, and ensure that the room is not used again for the rest of the day. If this is unavoidable, cover the talisman with a cloth or place it in a box. However, leave it in the room until the following morning.

CONCENTRATION METHOD ONE

This is a simple and highly effective method, but it takes a few days to complete. Twice a day, preferably in the morning and evening, hold your talisman in your cupped hands and concentrate all your energies on the talisman. Focus on what you want it to do for you. Concentrate for as long as possible, but stop as soon as your mind starts wandering. Place the talisman in a safe place, preferably wrapped in silk, until you are ready to do it again. Repeat for as many days as necessary; you will know when the talisman has been fully charged as it will gain a distinctive energy when you hold it in your cupped hands. Once this has been achieved, the talisman is ready for use.

CONCENTRATION METHOD TWO

This method is quicker than the previous one, but you need good powers of concentration to do it effectively. Place a white candle on an altar. The candle is unlit at the start of the process.

Hold your talisman between the palms of your hands, and stand in front of the altar. Rub your hands together gently while thinking of your need for the talisman. Look at your hands as you do this. Pause for a moment or two, and then say, "I charge you with divine energy." This should be said loudly, with as much force and passion as possible. Continue to rub the talisman gently, while you think about the services it will provide for you. After a minute or so, say, "I charge you with divine energy," using even more power, if possible. Repeat this four or five times.

You will know when to stop, as you will receive a response from the talisman. It might become warm in your hands, or you may feel energy radiating from it. When you experience this, place the talisman on your altar in front of the candle. Take three deep breaths and light the candle. When the candle is well lit, pass the talisman through the smoke several times while saying, "You are now charged and empowered for my use. This sacred smoke is to purify and strengthen you for [whatever purpose you have in mind]. Thank you." Pause for a few seconds. "Thank you." Pause again. "Thank you."

Blow out the candle and carry on with your day. Your talisman is now ready for use.

ASSOCIATION METHOD

This method involves placing your talisman in a container with other objects that relate to your desire. If you have made a talisman to attract wealth, for instance, you could place it in a container full of coins, jewelry, and other signs of wealth and abundance. If your talisman is to attract love, place it in a container full of signs of love. This could include rose petals, photographs of people in love, wedding rings, and so on.

Twice a day, for three days, hold the container and think about the task you are charging the talisman to accomplish. After three days, take the talisman out of the container and hold it between the palms of your hands. Think about the task again, and see if the talisman responds. You may feel a warmness between your hands, or perhaps just a sense of awareness that the talisman is fully charged. If you do not receive a response, replace the talisman in the container and start the process again.

PENDULUM METHOD

The pendulum is an extremely useful psychic tool and has almost unlimited capabilities. A pendulum is a small weight attached to a length of thread or chain. The ideal weight is three or four ounces, and most people find that a thread of between three and six inches works well. If you are right-handed hold the thread between the thumb and first finger of your right hand and let the weight hang freely. Left-handed people should do the same using their left hand. It can be helpful to rest the elbow of the arm holding the pendulum on a table. Stop the movement of the weight with your free hand, and then ask the pendulum to move in a direction that indicates "yes." The pendulum may take a minute or so to move initially, but will then move backwards and forwards, or from side to side, or perhaps revolve in a circular movement, either clockwise or counterclockwise.

Once the pendulum has told you which movement means "yes," you can stop the movement and then ask it for a "no" movement. Once you have ascertained this, you can then find out which movements indicate "I don't know" and "I don't want to answer."

These answers can be useful when working with talismans. Any time you wish, you can suspend a pendulum over your talisman and ask if it is fully charged. If the answer is negative, you can recharge the talisman.

You can also use your pendulum to charge your talisman. Place your talisman on a table, and hold your pendulum over it. Make the pendulum move in a clockwise direction so that it revolves around the talisman for sixty seconds. Stop the movements of the pendulum, and ask it if the talisman is ready to be charged. Hopefully, the answer will be positive. If you receive a negative response, put the pendulum and talisman away and try again at another time. You may find that you were trying to charge the talisman at an inauspicious time of day.

If you receive a positive response, make the pendulum move in a clockwise rotation again for a further sixty seconds. Stop the movement of the pendulum, and then gaze at the talisman while telling it what you require of it. You can speak silently or out loud. I prefer to say this out loud as I then hear what I say, which adds another dimension to the ritual. Keep the pendulum suspended either over or beside the talisman while doing this, but direct all your attention to the talisman. When you have finished talking, look at the pendulum again. If the talisman is charged, your pendulum will be moving in the "yes" direction. If it is doing this, give thanks, and then make the pendulum revolve around the talisman again for a further sixty seconds. The talisman is now ready for use. If you receive any other response from the pendulum, focus again on the talisman, repeating your desires and need for the talisman to become fully charged. Keep on doing this until your pendulum gives a positive response.

PURIFICATION IN FIRE METHOD

Purification by fire, or, more correctly, by smoke, is a frequently used method for charging talismans. You can use smoke from a candle or incense. Place the source of smoke on an altar and stand in front of it, holding your talisman in your cupped hands. Focus on your talisman and what you are charging it for; then pass it through the smoke as many times as feels right for you. If you are charging an astrological talisman pass it through the smoke the number of times that relate to the particular planet (as indicated on the facing page).

- Saturn: 3
- Jupiter: 4
- Mars: 5
- Sun: 6
- Venus: 7
- Mercury: 8
- Moon: 9

Keep focusing on your talisman as you do this. Some people like to finish this method of charging their talismans by adding the other elements of water, air, and earth. This is done by sprinkling a few drops of water on the talisman, again while concentrating you energies on it. Follow this by breathing on your talisman to add the air element.[2] For an astrological talisman, breathe on it the same number of times that you used when passing it through the flame. Finally, sprinkle a little salt on the talisman to add earth.

Hold your talisman as high as you can with both hands and give thanks. Your talisman is now charged and ready for use.

Destroying a Talisman

The ancient Egyptians believed that the magical properties of their amulets would last forever.[3] This was because even amulets made to be worn by living persons were ultimately intended to be worn on the mummy in the tomb to help the wearer in the afterlife.

However, there might be occasions when you do not want these magical energies to continue indefinitely. The most common example of this is a talisman that has been constructed for a specific purpose. Once the goal has been achieved there is no further need for the talisman. Consequently, it has to be deactivated or destroyed. Unless the materials used are valuable, such as gold or silver, it is generally better to destroy the talisman after thanking it for helping you.

It can be helpful to make a small ritual of this, to thank the talisman formally and to say goodbye. If the talisman can be burned, place a lighted candle on an altar, and stand in front of it holding the talisman in your cupped hands. Turn to the east and bow. Do the same for south, west, and north, and then turn to face the candle again. Say to the talisman, "Thank you for your help. I greatly appreciate it. However, you have fulfilled your purpose, and I must let you go. Thank you once again."

Hold the talisman as high as you can for a moment, and then burn it in the flame of the candle. You are likely to feel genuine sorrow as your talisman burns. This is perfectly natural, as you are saying goodbye to a friend. Watch it burn and leave the ashes in front of the candle for an hour or so before disposing of them.

If the talisman is made of a substance that cannot be burned, go through the same process of thanking it and saying goodbye. Then break it, if possible, and bury it in the ground. If it is valuable, and you want to keep the talisman for some reason, go through the same process of thanking it for three days in a row. This will remove all the talismanic influences. You should test this with a pendulum (see page 110). If the pendulum tells you some influences remain, repeat the procedure and test again until the pendulum tells you all the influences have gone.

crystals & gemstones

CRYSTALS AND GEMSTONES have always been associated with amulets and talismans. This is because of the special properties that these stones are believed to possess. An ancient cuneiform inscription includes a list of stones that assist conception and birth, and induce friendship and hatred.[1] The ancient Babylonians believed that everything was subject to the influence of heavenly powers, and that stones had a special place in astrology, as their colors naturally became associated with the colors of the planets. As they also related different metals to each planet, amulets and talismans that were made of the correct metal and colored stone for a specific astrological or magical purpose were popular. The combined energy of both stone and metal meant that amulets and talismans were more than mere decorations; they could be put to more important uses. The jewel necklace of Princess Sat-Hathor-Ant, for instance, was strung with golden lion's claws to act as a protective amulet.

Over time, people have also come to realize that all stones resonate at different vibratory levels. When a stone strikes a special "chord" with us we are either attracted or repelled by it. The right chord makes us feel in balance, while the wrong chord makes us feel uncomfortable. When we wear the correct gemstones we feel good about ourselves and are able to maintain balance in every area of our lives. This works in two ways, because, obviously, we impart our own energies to the gemstone as well. Thoughts are living forces and whatever it is we think about is transferred to the jewelry we wear.

History

It appears that people adorned themselves with earrings and necklaces long before they considered wearing clothes.[2] Necklaces have been found that date back to the Stone Age. Primitive people were apparently intrigued by anything colorful or attractive and fashioned such objects into jewelry. It wasn't long before there was scarcely a part of the body that could not be decorated with precious stones. Crowns, diadems, tiaras, hairpins, and combs decorated the hair. Earrings, nose rings, and lip rings decorated the rest of the head. Armlets, bracelets and rings adorned the arms and hands. Thigh bracelets, ankle bracelets, toe rings, and buckles decorated the legs and feet. A variety of brooches, breastplates, stomachers, and belts decorated the torso.

By the fourth millennium B.C.E., the Egyptians were using emery powder to polish precious stones, and one millennium later they had the ability to cut, polish, and engrave precious stones. Amethyst, beryl, carnelian, chalcedony, garnet, jasper, and rock crystal were commonly treated in this way. All quartz crystal was revered, and even cups were made from it, enabling people to receive benefit every time they drank from them. Precious stones do not deteriorate the way almost everything else does, and so many examples of these can be found in museums around the world.

Reverence for gems did not end with death. Precious jewelry was buried with the dead to aid the person's passage to the next world. For instance, lapis lazuli carved into the shape of an eye was considered a powerful amulet for the deceased. Jewelry in the shape of scarabs was also common. Scarabs symbolized reincarnation, making it a popular talisman for both the living and the dead.

There is also evidence that ancient people tried to harness the power of gems on a larger scale. The bases of the pyramids are made of granite containing up to forty percent quartz crystal. It is possible that the pyramids were intended to be powerful generators of energy, which could be harnessed by priests for healing purposes.[3]

Adding the written word to talismanic gems also seems to have been an early practice. It appears that the engraving of stones began in southern Mesopotamia. A strong and powerful word or two engraved on a stone made it much more potent and effective as a talisman or amulet.

Gem stones were highly prized by the ancient Greeks and Romans, and wealthy people collected them with a passion. Alexandria was the center of the jewel trade, and merchants from Athens and Rome would go there to bid for fine specimens to take home and resell. Rivalry and jealousy amongst collectors was common, and Mark Antony exiled a senator named Nonius when he refused to give him a certain gem, valued at twenty thousand sesterces (more than a million dollars in today's currency).[4]

Much of our knowledge of the early history of gem stones comes from the writings of Theophrastus (circa. 371–287 B.C.E.) and Pliny the Elder (23–79 C.E.). Later on, we are indebted to the writings of Marco Polo (1254 –1324) and Jean-Baptiste Tavernier (1605–1689) who made a fortune trading in precious stones. Many other authors wrote about the curative powers of gemstones, including Aristotle, Hildegard von Bingen, and St. Isadore of Seville. Boëtius de Boot, court physician to Rudolph II of Germany, wrote about good and bad angels who were able to enter gemstones and protect them from danger.[5]

In medieval times, a lady would present her knight with a precious stone, set in the hilt of his sword, before he headed off on a dangerous mission. The choice of stone depended on the particular qualities the lady wanted to give to her knight. A diamond, for instance, would give him courage, while an amethyst would promote sobriety.[6]

Gems have also had specific cosmic and zodiacal correspondences for centuries, but it wasn't until the middle of the sixteenth century that gemstones became associated with specific months. People started buying gemstone amulets and talismans that related to their month of birth. These stones were originally chosen because they related to the twelve gemstones on the Breastplate of Aaron, the High Priest of Israel.

Aaron was the older brother of Moses and served as high priest for forty years. The holy garments he wore were magnificent. In addition to the breastplate, he wore a waistcoat, robe, coat, girdle, and turban, all made of the finest materials. The breastplate was some nine inches square and had twelve gem stones set on it in gold filigree. Each of these gems had the name of one of the twelve tribes of Israel engraved on it. When he wore this breastplate, Aaron was able to receive revelations from God. All of Aaron's apparel is described in the twenty-eighth chapter of Exodus.

There has been much discussion about the twelve gems that Aaron had on his breastplate. The gems mentioned in the King James translation of the Bible are sardius, topaz, carbuncle, emerald, sapphire, diamond, ligure, agate, amethyst, beryl, onyx, and jasper. Many scholars have questioned the accuracy of this translation, and different translations of the Bible have suggested different stones. Here is a compilation of the most commonly mentioned gems for each of the twelve stones.

1. Sardius, carnelian, red feldspar, red jasper, ruby
2. Topaz, peridot, serpentine
3. Carbuncle (ruby), emerald, green feldspar, rock crystal
4. Emerald, garnet, ruby
5. Sapphire, lapis lazuli
6. Diamond, jade, green jasper, onyx, sardonyx
7. Ligure, hyacinth, jacinth, amber, sapphire, agate
8. Agate, ruby
9. Amethyst, blue or purple quartz
10. Beryl, chrysolite, quartz, yellow jasper, topaz
11. Onyx, malachite, beryl, turquoise
12. Jasper, jade

However, much of this is conjecture, and the suggested gemstones for each month have changed slightly as time went on.

In the first century c.e., the Roman writer Flavius Josephus wrote about the twelve gemstones on the breastplate and associated them with the twelve months and the twelve signs of the zodiac.[7] However, at that time people did not wear a single stone that was associated with their date of birth. Instead, wealthy Romans wore all twelve stones in whatever combination they desired—often wearing several at a time or simply the relevant one for the month they were in.

For almost fifteen hundred years, people wore gemstones as amulets or talismans, rather than as a stone that related to their sign or month of birth. It is believed that the Jewish people in seventeenth-century Poland were the first to wear gems that represented the month in which they were born. The list of birthstones that they used is as follows.

- January: garnet
- February: amethyst
- March: bloodstone
- April: diamond
- May: emerald
- June: agate
- July: cornelian
- August: sardonyx
- September: chrysolite (better known today as peridot)
- October: opal
- November: topaz
- December: turquoise

In 1912, the American National Retail Jewelers Association looked at all of the lists of birthstones that were available at that time and tried to create a list that would satisfy everyone. Part of the reason for this was that some of the original stones were hard to find or were no longer considered attractive. Over the years, alexandrite and citrine were added to the list, and blue zircon replaced lapis lazuli. In 1938, the American Gem Society approved this list for its members. In 1952, the National Jewelers Association also accepted a variation of the original list. Consequently, the "accepted" stones for each month are as follows.

- January: garnet
- February: amethyst
- March: bloodstone, aquamarine
- April: diamond
- May: emerald
- June: pearl, moonstone, alexandrite
- July: ruby
- August: sardonyx, peridot
- September: sapphire
- October: opal, pink tourmaline
- November: topaz, citrine
- December: turquoise, zircon

Naturally, not everyone is happy with this list, and a number of variations have been produced. There is no doubt, though, that these stones can act as beneficial amulets for the people who wear them, as long as they have faith in their effectiveness.

Something these early jewelers failed to take into account is that most people prefer to wear a stone that relates to their astrological sign as opposed to their birth month. It is possible to do this to a certain extent by simply moving each gem forward a few weeks. This works perfectly for some of the stones, but not for others. For example, bloodstone, the stone for March, fits in perfectly with the sign of Aries (approximately March 21 through April 20). Bloodstone, as mentioned before, was used as a talisman by soldiers and is naturally associated with Mars, the god of war. Mars happens to be the ruler of Aries, making this a perfect match.

Not surprisingly, experts differ as to the correct stones for each birth sign. Here is a list of suggested gem stones for each of the astrological signs.

- Aries: bloodstone, diamond, jasper, ruby
- Taurus: sapphire, turquoise, emerald, lapis lazuli, carnelian
- Gemini: agate, pearl, moonstone, alexandrite, citrine
- Cancer: emerald, moonstone, ruby, olivine
- Leo: agate, diamond, sardonyx, peridot

- Virgo: jade, sapphire, carnelian, jasper
- Libra: opal, lapis lazuli, tourmaline, emerald, aventurine, jade
- Scorpio: beryl, aquamarine, topaz, citrine, garnet
- Sagittarius: topaz, jacinth, peridot, turquoise, zircon
- Capricorn: garnet, ruby, malachite, black onyx, jet
- Aquarius: amethyst, garnet, malachite, turquoise, zircon
- Pisces: aquamarine, bloodstone, amethyst

If one of the stones for your sign appeals to you, it would make a good amulet or talisman. However, there is no reason why you shouldn't simply select a stone that appeals to you for any reason, and use that.

Choosing a Stone by Numerology

We can use numerology when choosing a gemstone. Everything that can be named has a numerological value. (We'll see this in more detail in chapters to come.) Consequently, every gemstone can be looked at numerologically to see how it relates to you.

Each number has a meaning. Here are brief keywords for each number.

1   Independence, attainment

2   Cooperation, harmony, diplomacy

3   Creative self-expression, joys of life

4   System, order, restrictions, hard work

5   Freedom, variety

6   Home and family responsibilities

7   Analysis, wisdom, spirituality

8   Material freedom

9   Humanitarianism

There are also two master numbers, eleven and twenty-two. These are more highly evolved than the other numbers, and there is always a degree of nervous tension associated with them. These numbers belong to people who are old souls.

11   Illumination, inspiration

22   Master builder

In numerology, four numbers comprise your basic makeup. These are your Life Path, Expression, Soul Urge, and Day of Birth.

LIFE PATH

The most important of these is your Life Path, which reveals your purpose in life. Your Life Path number is derived from your full date of birth, reduced down to a single digit. My date of birth is December 9, 1946. To work out my Life Path number, we have to turn these numbers into a sum in the following manner:

12– Month
9– Day
1946– Year

$$12 + 9 + 1946 = 1967$$

We then add up these individual digits

$$1 + 9 + 6 + 7 = 23$$

and keep on doing this until we arrive at a single digit:

$$2 + 3 = 5.$$

My Life Path number is five.

There is one exception to this. If, at any time while you are reducing the numbers down to a single digit you arrive at an eleven or twenty-two, the two Master numbers, you stop reducing at that point. Here is an example, using my wife Margaret's date of birth.

2 – Month
29 – Day
1944 – Year

$$2 + 29 + 1944 = 1975$$

and then

$$1 + 9 + 7 + 5 = 22.$$

As this is a Master number, we do not reduce the total down to four. Margaret's Life Path number is twenty-two.

Margaret's date of birth also shows why we need to create a sum in this way, rather than simply adding up the numbers in a straight line. If we do that with Margaret's date of birth, we lose the Master number

$$2 \text{ (month)} + 2 + 9 \text{ (day)} + 1 + 9 + 4 + 4 = 31,$$

and then

$$3 + 1 = 4.$$

With a Life Path number of five, I have had to learn to use my time wisely and not waste too much of it. The keywords for five are freedom and variety. That means that if I am not careful, I will overindulge in the delights of freedom and variety and not achieve anything. In my case, it took me many years to learn this lesson.

Margaret's lesson is much more difficult. She has a Master number for her Life Path. This means that everyone is probably aware of her superior capabilities, except perhaps her. She needs to find something worthy of her capabilities—a magnificent obsession, perhaps—and then follow it through.

EXPRESSION

The Expression number reveals your natural abilities. It comes from your full name at birth, reduced to a single digit or Master number. We do this by turning each letter of our name into a number using the chart below (for more on this chart, see 177).

1	2	3	4	5	6	7	8	9
A	B	C	D	E	F	G	H	I
J	K	L	M	N	O	P	Q	R
S	T	U	V	W	X	Y	Z	

Here is my full name with the numerological values underneath:

RICHARD   EDWARD   WEBSTER
9938194   545194   5521259

Each word is reduced separately by adding the individual digits.

43 28 29

and then again to

7 10 11

and finally

7 1 11.

(Note that eleven is a Master number and is not reduced). The three reduced numbers are then added

$$7 + 1 + 11 = 19$$

and added again (unless the previous sum is a Master number)

$$1 + 9 = 10$$

and added again, if necessary,

$$1 + 0 = 1.$$

My Expression number is one.

SOUL URGE

The Soul Urge is also known as the heart's desire and shows what you want to achieve in this lifetime. It is a person's motivating factor. It is the total of all the vowels in your name at birth, again reduced down to a single digit or Master number. This is complicated, because *Y* can be both a vowel and a consonant. If it is pronounced, as in the name Yolanda, it is considered a consonant. If it is not pronounced (as in Kaye), or acts as a vowel (as in Lynda), it is considered a vowel.

RICHARD		EDWARD		WEBSTER	
9	1	5	1	5	5

The reduction would go as follows.

10 6 10

1 6 1

1 + 6 + 1 = 8.

My Soul Urge is eight.

DAY OF BIRTH

This is the easiest of the four numbers to determine. It is the day of the month you were born on reduced to a single digit—except, of course for people born on the eleventh, twenty-second, or twenty-ninth of any month. People born on the twenty-ninth have an eleven day of birth number. I was born on the ninth, so have a nine day of birth. Margaret was born on the twenty-ninth, which gives her an eleven Day-of-Birth number.

PUTTING IT TOGETHER

We have looked at the four main numbers of numerology in descending order of importance. Your Life Path represents forty percent of your total makeup, Expression thirty percent, Soul Urge twenty percent, and Day of Birth ten percent. In my case, my numbers are five, one, eight, and nine.

Because these are my numbers and are an integral part of my makeup, I will get on well with anyone who shares one or more of my numbers. I will also relate well with any gemstone or crystal that vibrates to these same numbers. Here is an example.

Aquamarine

1831419955

46

10

1

An aquamarine amulet or talisman would work well for me, as we share the same Expression number.

Here is another example.

Moonstone

66   6 5

23

5

A moonstone amulet or talisman would also work for me, as it has a five Soul Urge, which connects with my five Life Path.

Alexandrite

13561549925

50

5

Alexandrite has an Expression number of five, and this relates well with my Life Path of five. Sardonyx has a five Soul Urge (the Y is considered a vowel), as does citrine. Ruby has a one Soul Urge. Opal has an Expression number of eight. Turquoise harmonizes with me on two levels: a one Expression and an eight Soul Urge.

Which of these gems would be the best for me? At first glance, it would seem that turquoise would be the best as it connects with me on two levels. However, it all depends on what I would be using the gem for. If I were to use it as part of a talisman to help me achieve my life's purpose, I would likely choose alexandrite, moonstone, or sardonyx, as they have a five vibration, which is the same as my Life Path. If I wanted a gem to help me achieve a specific goal or to assert my independence, I would choose aquamarine or turquoise, as both of these gems have an Expression number of one. If my goal were a financial one, I would definitely choose turquoise, as eight is the number that vibrates with money.

Choosing a Gemstone by Color

We can also add color to the equation when deciding on a particular gemstone. The numbers we used in numerology can also help us choose the right colors. Here are the colors that relate to each of the numbers.

1   Red

2   Orange

3   Yellow

4   Green

5   Blue

6   Indigo

7   Violet

8   Pink

9   Clear

The Master numbers eleven and twenty-two relate to silver and gold, respectively. (Now you know why the saints in stained glass windows always have gold auras.)

As you know, my numbers are five, one, eight, and nine. This means that I could choose an amulet or talisman that is blue (five), red (one), pink (eight), or clear (nine).

I've included below some of the key colored-stone characteristics.

RED (1)

Red stones are passionate and energetic. They can motivate you to attempt things you would never normally contemplate. Red is the color of blood, and red energy stimulates every aspect of our being. Ruby, garnet, and red jasper are good examples.

ORANGE (2)

Orange stones relate to close relationships and the satisfaction of a job well done. Citrine, carnelian, and orange sapphire are good examples.

YELLOW (3)

Yellow stones relate to expressing the joys of life. They are fun-loving, joyful, mischievous, and enjoy company. If you are feeling lonely, carry a yellow stone around with you and see how many people you attract. Yellow energy also stimulates the intellect. Yellow beryl and topaz are good examples.

GREEN (4)

Green stones relate to regeneration, nurturing, hard work, and accomplishment. They create the determination, persistence, and energy to achieve a demanding task. Emerald, peridot, jade, and tourmaline are good examples.

BLUE (5)

Blue stones provide perception and the ability to visualize what can be accomplished. Sapphire, tourmaline, lapis lazuli, and iolite are good examples. Lapis lazuli is sometimes called the Seer's Stone, because it effectively opens the doors to intuition and foresight.

INDIGO (6)

Indigo stones relate to love and caring for others, particularly the people you are closest to. Amethyst is a good example.

VIOLET (7)

Violet stones relate to the higher consciousness and provide wisdom and spiritual truths. Purple ruby, garnet, and siberite tourmaline are good examples.

PINK (8)

Pink stones provide the stimulation and energy that allows growth to occur. Rubellite tourmaline, rose beryl, and rose quartz are good examples.

CLEAR (9)

Clear stones represent pure energy, because they contain the energy and potential of all the other colors. Clear quartz is an example. Clear stones are nurturing, caring, loving, and unlimited in their potential.

SILVER (11)

Silver stones are superficially passive and peaceful. However, they possess enormous potential and, when properly harnessed and motivated, provide sufficient stimulation and energy to allow enormous progress to be made. Hematite is a good example.

GOLD (22)

Gold stones are active, motivated, and ambitious. They enhance the potential of any other stone and also work well on their own. Gold should be used when you are aiming for the sky. Gold knows no limits. Wear it over your heart and aim as high as you dare. Pyrite, pyrite-sun, and tiger's-eye are good examples.

chapter 6

Gemstones in the East

I started my study of amulets and talismans while in the Far East. The sheer number of talismans that people wear in Thailand, for instance, is extraordinary by Western standards. However, they serve a valuable purpose, and people would not continue to wear them unless they felt they were receiving some benefit.

As we might expect, amulets and talismans can be found among the relics of the earliest Eastern civilizations. Jade objects dating back to the Neolithic era have been found in China. These were used in religious ceremonies and were also worn as protective amulets.[8] Indian mythology tells the story of a fabulous ruby called Syamantaka that gave brilliance to Surya, the sun god. One day Surya gave the jewel to a human, King Satrajit, and this caused enormous problems. Syamantaka was an amazing gem that gave more good to people who did good and more evil to people who committed evil deeds.

The famous Kalpa Tree was created by Hindu poets as the ultimate gift to the gods. It had leaves of coral, shoots of emeralds, a trunk of diamonds, topaz, and chrysoberyl, and roots of sapphire. Pearls hung from its branches, and it bore fruit of rubies.

There is an ancient and highly venerated item of Hindu jewelry known as the Nav-Ratna ring. The words *nav ratna* means "nine gemstones." The Nav-Ratna ring is worn on the ring finger of the right hand. The back side of the setting is kept open to allow the gems to remain in contact with the skin. The stones are fixed in position in three rows. Topaz, chrysoberyl (a type of cat's-eye), and emerald are in the first row. Sapphire, ruby, and diamond make up the second row, and the final row contains hessonite (garnet), coral, and pearl. These gems align all of the planetary forces to provide good luck, protection, and aid for whoever wears it.

Like all things, the degree of benefit the wearer receives is dependent on the quality of the gems. Inferior stones can cause harm, rather than benefit to the wearer. It is better to substitute similarly colored gemstones of good quality, than use poor quality gems of the proper type. There are references in the Vedic scriptures about the inauspicious effects of imperfect gemstones, and the beneficial effects of good quality stones.[9]

Throughout history, people in India have worn jewelry as an essential part of their attire. It is just as popular today as it was thousands of years ago. Nose rings, earrings, necklaces, bangles, arm bands, finger rings, belts, ankle bracelets, and toe rings can be seen everywhere. It is likely that people in India have been wearing jewelry for at least five thousand years.[10]

Some of this jewelry is purely ornamental, but a great deal is worn for talismanic purposes. For instance, it is common to see intertwining cobras on rings and bracelets. In Hindu mythology, the earth's mineral wealth is guarded by *nagas*, who are serpent gods. These snakes protect their wearers from harm, and they are also believed to provide an antidote for poison.

SYSTEMS FOR CHOOSING EASTERN GEMS

The late Dr. L. R. Chawdhri was a well-known palmist in New Delhi. At the end of his consultations, he frequently gave his clients a semiprecious stone, telling them it would bring them good luck. I was intrigued at the way he did this and began following his system in my own practice.

He told me that there were eighty-four kinds of stones that could be used as amulets or talismans or for decorative purposes. However, for practical purposes, nine gems (the Nav-Ratna gems) cover almost every possibility, and it was one of these that he gave to his clients.

He gave his clients a gem that was determined by the person's Life Path number or day of birth. It was important that a ring made from this particular gem was in an open setting in order to to allow it to make contact with the skin. The ring should be worn on the right ring finger. The purpose of the gem is to enhance the person's good qualities as well as eliminate some of the negative. The gem also makes the person's progress through the ups and downs of life that much easier. Dr. Chawdhri's gem choices for Life Path number and date of birth follow.

(It is believed that all rings, except for ruby, should be placed in raw milk for three hours before being worn for the first time. This is to remove any impurities that may be present. Ruby rings should be placed in lemon juice for three hours.)

Life Path numbers

You will recall that the Life Path number is determined by adding up the month, day and year of birth, and then reducing the total down to a single digit, or a Master Number.

1   Ruby, topaz

2   Moonstone, cat's-eye, tiger's-eye

3   Amethyst

4   Golden-red garnet

5   Diamond

6   Emerald, peridot

7   Moonstone, cat's-eye, tiger's-eye

8   Blue sapphire, lapis lazuli

9   Coral

11 Pearl

22 Blue aquamarine

People born on the 1st, 10th, 19th, or 28th

These people should wear a ring containing either red coral, red opal, ruby, or yellow or gold topaz. However, if the total of the month, day, and year reduced down to a single digit is two, four, seven, or eight, ruby should not be worn.

People born on the first, tenth, nineteenth, and twenty-eighth come under the influence of the sun. Consequently, they have high standards and ideals and desire success. Their destiny is to be in any field where their leadership skills can be allowed full play.

People born on the 2nd, 11th, 20th, or 29th

These people should wear jewelry containing cat's-eye, green opal, jade, moonstone, pearl, or tiger's-eye.

People born on these days come under the influence of the moon. They are gentle, caring, nurturing, and intuitive. They enjoy helping others and work well in fields where their empathy can be used.

People born on the 3rd, 12th, 21st, or 30th

People born on these days should wear jewelry of amethyst, coral, emerald, or topaz.

These people come under the influence of Jupiter. They are honest, affectionate, and sharing. They are quietly ambitious and are prepared to work tirelessly for whatever it is they want. They do well in business.

People born on the 4th, 13th, 22nd, or 31st

People born on these days should wear jewelry of blue aquamarine, diamond, garnet, light-blue sapphire, or reddish-brown-and-gray opal.

These people come under the influence of Uranus. They are hard-working and do not like being told what to do. They express their thoughts well but are not good at listening to the ideas of others, even when they have requested them.

People born on the 5th, 14th, or 23rd

People born on these days should wear diamond, white sapphire, or zircon.

These people are under the influence of Mercury. They are quick-witted and enjoy beautiful surroundings and attractive possessions. They prefer mentally stimulating work to manual labor and generally have a talent for making money so they can surround themselves with the good things of life.

People born on the 6th, 15th, or 24th

People born on these days should wear beryl, emerald, green aquamarine, green opal, or peridot. However, if the sum of their month, day, and year of birth reduced down to a single digit is three, they should wear golden topaz or yellow sapphire instead.

People born on the sixteenth, fifteenth, or twenty-forth are under the influence of Venus. They enjoy helping others but are selective when it comes to making friends. They enjoy the pleasures of life and are prepared to work to earn the money first. They dislike idleness.

People born on the 7th, 16th, or 25th

People born on these days should wear cat's-eye, moonstone, white opal, pearl, or tiger's-eye.

These people are under the influence of Neptune. They are interested in a wide range of subjects but do not always share these enthusiasms with others. They work well in fields that require research and enjoy seeking out hidden truths. They are naturally intuitive and can sum up other people at a glance.

People born on the 8th, 17th, or 26th

People born on these days should wear blue sapphire, lapis lazuli, or reddish-brown-and-gray opal.

These people are under the influence of Saturn. They are hard workers who achieve their goals. They are honest, stubborn, determined, and resourceful. They are practical people who keep their feet firmly on the ground.

People born on the 9th, 18th, or 27th

People born on these days should wear coral, garnet, red opal, ruby, or a Nav-Ratna ring (containing all nine gems). However, if the sum of their month, day, and year of birth reduces down to two or seven, they should wear cat's-eye, moonstone, pearl or tiger's-eye instead.

People born on the ninth, eighteenth, or twenty-seventh are under the influence of Mars. These people are prepared to try anything, and they do it all with good humor. They enjoy both physical and mental endeavors and need a challenge to keep them interested. They have a wide range of interests and can influence others by their example.

ZODIACAL RINGS

Astrological talismans are called *kavacas* in India. They are used to influence the cosmic vibrations of the universe, and to improve every aspect of the lives of the people wearing them.

Hindu astrology differs in many ways from Western astrology in that it is a sidereal rather than tropical system. Sidereal astrology has been used for thousands of years in the East. It is based on the study of the celestial bodies, the earth being one of these. The tropical system of astrology that we use in the West is based on the placement of the sun in relation to the earth. The most obvious difference to someone comparing the two systems is that the sun signs have slightly different dates in both systems. In Eastern astrology, Aries runs from April 13 to May 14, while in Western astrology it runs from March 21 to April 21.

Not surprisingly, as well as different dates for the signs, they also have a different selection of birthstones. As in the West, there is considerable disagreement about the correct birthstones for each sign. I have listed here the most common choices. In each case, the first one listed is the one I was taught originally.

- Aries (April 15 to May 14): red coral, ruby, bloodstone, red jasper
- Taurus (May 15 to June 14): diamond, coral, emerald, golden topaz
- Gemini (June 15 to July 14): emerald, aquamarine
- Cancer (July 15 to August 14): pearl, emerald, moonstone

- Leo (August 15 to September 14): ruby, amber
- Virgo (September 15 to October 14): emerald, pink jasper, turquoise, zircon
- Libra (October 15 to November 14): diamond, opal
- Scorpio (November 15 to December 14): red coral, agate, garnet, topaz
- Sagittarius (December 15 to January 14): yellow sapphire, amethyst
- Capricorn (January 15 to February 14): blue sapphire, beryl, jet, smoky quartz
- Aquarius (February 15 to March 14): zircon, blue sapphire
- Pisces (March 15 to April 14): cat's-eye, aquamarine, diamond, jade

GEMSTONES FOR THE PLANETS

In the East, it is believed that you can improve the quality of your life by using gemstones to enhance the planetary positions in your sidereal horoscope.

If a planet is in an unfortunate position in your horoscope, a specific gemstone can be worn to rectify the problem. In fact, two gemstones should be worn: one to ward off the negativity of an unfortunate planetary placement and the other to symbolize the person's ruling planet.

Here is a list of the correct gemstones for each planet. Listed first is the correct stone, followed by suggested alternate stones.

- Sun: ruby, red garnet, rubellite, red spinel, red tourmaline
- Moon: pearl, moonstone
- Mars: coral, bloodstone, carnelian
- Mercury: emerald, green diopside, jade, peridot, green tourmaline
- Jupiter: topaz, yellow beryl, citrine, heliodor, yellow sapphire, yellow tourmaline
- Venus: diamond, quartz, white sapphire, white topaz, white zircon
- Saturn: sapphire, amethyst, cordierite, blue spinel
- Rahu: orange garnet, spessartite, orange zircon
- Ketu: cat's-eye, beryl, fibrolite

Rahu and Ketu are considered to be *aprakasha,* or "shadowy planets," and are often referred to as the dragon's head and dragon's tail. In Hindu astrology, Rahu and Ketu reflect the qualities of whatever sign they happen to be in.

GEMSTONES FOR EACH DAY OF THE WEEK

You may also choose to wear the correct stone for every day of the week. Alternatively, you might choose to wear a stone that represents your day of birth. In the East, the sapta-ratna talisman is often worn. It contains the seven gems that correspond to each day of the week.

Sunday
Ruled by the sun. All yellow or gold gems. Examples include amber, carnelian, gold citrine, and gold topaz.

Monday
Ruled by the moon. All white stones. Examples include moonstone, opal, and pearl.

Tuesday
Ruled by Mars. All red stones. Examples include bloodstone, coral, garnet, red jasper, and ruby.

Wednesday
Ruled by Mercury. All blue stones. Examples include aquamarine, lapis lazuli, sapphire, sodalite, blue topaz, and turquoise.

Thursday
Ruled by Jupiter. All purple stones. Examples include amethyst and fluorite.

Friday
Ruled by Venus. All green stones. Examples include chrysoprase, emerald, green jade, malachite, peridot, and green tourmaline.

Saturday
Ruled by Saturn. All black and white stones. Examples include diamond and smoky quartz.

STONES FOR EACH FINGER
Each finger is connected with a different part of the body's central nervous system. Consequently, it is believed in India that wearing certain rings on specific fingers can help cure problems and illnesses. The thumb does not confer any benefit and is not used.

First finger
The first finger, or index finger, is ruled by Jupiter. It also represents the stomach and respiratory system. To help cure problems in these areas, rings of moonstone, pearl, or yellow sapphire should be worn on this finger.

Second finger
The second finger is ruled by Saturn. It represents the brain, liver, and intestines. For problems in these areas rings of white coral, diamond, emerald, moonstone, pearl, blue sapphire, or white zircon should be worn.

Third finger
The third finger is ruled by the sun. It represents the kidneys and the circulation of the blood. Rings of ruby, red coral, cat's eye, moonstone, pearl, yellow sapphire, and topaz can be worn on this finger to aid problems in these areas.

Fourth finger

The fourth finger is ruled by Mercury. It represents the genitals, legs, and feet. For problems in these areas, rings of lapis lazuli and blue sapphire should be worn.

Talismanic Gemstones

Most scholars believe that people began wearing gems for talismanic, rather than adornment, purposes. Consequently, jewelry came from magic, and was originally designed to repel negative energies. Certain gems were found to be more beneficial than others, and a small number became the gemstones of choice when it came to the making of talismans. Here are some of the more popular ones.

AMBER

Amber can be worn by anyone and is believed to bring the wearer closer to God. It is also worn to help relieve breathing problems.

BLACK TOURMALINE

Black tourmaline is believed to be the most powerful of the black gems. It acts as a protective shield against negative energies and psychic attack. It also helps us turn our hopes and dreams into reality.

BLOODSTONE

Bloodstone is believed to cure anemia and promote strong bone growth. It is often worn by children to help them become healthy and vigorous.

CRYSTAL

Crystal balances the aura and eliminates blocked energy. It also aids intuition.

DIAMOND

Diamond eliminates negative thoughts and encourages a positive outlook on life. It counteracts poison. It aids spiritual growth.

JADE

Jade is worn to attract good luck and wealth. It is especially beneficial for people who have a lucky number of two, six, or seven. (Most people will name a single-digit number when asked for a lucky number. Usually, this is a number chosen at random, but sometimes people select their lucky numbers using numerology. Consequently, they usually use their Life Path, Expression, or Soul Urge numbers as their lucky number.)

MOONSTONE

Moonstone encourages calmness and helps reduce and adverse effects of the emotions. It aids the lymphatic system.

It also restores endocrine imbalances in women. Moonstone enhances the female side of people's personalities.

OPAL

Opal helps balance the chakras and encourages spiritual growth. (The chakras are seven revolving circles of energy located alongside the spinal column inside the aura. They act like batteries and provide energy that can be utilized by the physical body.

PEARL

Pearl helps our inner growth, gently encouraging us to progress to a higher, more advanced level of spirituality.

SMOKY QUARTZ

Smoky quartz symbolizes the hidden, deeper truths and helps us to overcome procrastination and negative thoughts, so that we can develop physically, mentally, emotionally, and—particularly—spiritually.

Procuring Gemstones

Gemstones and crystals are easy to buy in large cities where there are specialist crystal stores, and most New Age shops have a small range of gems and crystals for sale. However, it is still not easy for people living in smaller centers to locate a good source of crystals. Fortunately, a large number of companies sell crystals and gemstones on the Internet. People who offer crystal workshops are another possibility, as they usually have a supply of reasonably priced crystals.

Whenever possible, you should choose your crystals yourself. There is no mystery to it. You might be attracted to the shape, color, size, or brilliance of a certain stone. If it appeals to you and the price is within your budget, buy it. It's exactly the same as buying clothes or food. A crystal that appeals to you might hold no interest to someone else. Naturally, the opposite also applies.

I use a variety of methods to select crystals. The look of a crystal is important, and sometimes my eye will be taken by one particular crystal in a display. I almost always buy a crystal that presents itself to me in this way. The second method is a form of psychometry. I hold a number of crystals, one at a time, and the "right" crystal for my needs will feel different to the others. I also use a pendulum to dowse for the right crystal. I think about my reasons for wanting a particular crystal while suspending my pendulum over a variety of crystals, one at a time. Invariably, my pendulum will tell me which one to choose. A friend of mine dowses for crystals with her hand. She holds the palm of her right hand over a selection of crystals, and says that her hand feels "sticky" when she's over the right crystal or gemstone. In effect, the right crystals choose you.

USING YOUR INTUITION

Most of the time, I will choose a stone by using my numbers or colors. However, sometimes I choose something totally different and usually have no idea why I did so. I may have walked into a store intending to buy, say, a blue tourmaline and left sixty minutes later with a white moonstone. This is because gemstones are incredibly powerful at enhancing one's psychic or intuitive abilities.

Consequently, when I am looking at gemstones and feel an intuitive response from a particular stone, I will almost always buy it, because the stone must have been sending me a message for a specific reason. I may feel that I have chosen a particular stone because I happened to like it, but, in reality, the stone chose me.

I find it helpful to have my particular need in mind when shopping for crystals or gemstones. I will have one or more stones in mind, ahead of time, but frequently end up buying something completely different to what I had intended.

It pays to allow plenty of time when shopping for gems. Sometimes the energies are subtle, and you will miss them if you are in a hurry. Everyone responds in a different way. A friend of mine hears the crystals talking to her. In fact, she says that she can hear them sing. Other people feel a tingling sensation in their fingers. For others, it's a sense of "knowing." Take whatever time is required for the stone to choose you.

How to Wear Gemstones

Talismanic gemstones can be worn in any way you wish. Usually, they are set in rings, but they can also be made into tie pins, bracelets, necklaces, and earrings, or they can be incorporated into other items of jewelry. Alternatively, they may be carried on the person in a small bag, wallet, or purse.

You may choose to wear them in a certain place because your body craves the energy they provide. A common example of this is wearing rings on the left hand, if you are right-handed. This is done subconsciously because the left-hand side of the body is weaker than the right, and wearing a crystal or gem on the left-hand side compensates for this. Naturally, if the person is left-handed, the ring would have to be worn on the right hand. Bracelets are often subconsciously placed on the correct side of the body for the same reason. Anklets serve the same function for the lower part of the body and help keep their wearers grounded. They also provide additional energy for the practical, everyday aspects of life.

Earrings help provide balance and harmony. As an aside, my mother-in-law suffered from tinnitus for many years. It disappeared completely as soon as she started wearing quartz crystal earrings.

Necklaces and pendants help eliminate blockages in the throat area. They can be extremely beneficial for people who have problems in expressing themselves clearly.

There are many valid reasons for wearing magical objects made of crystals or gemstones. Our ancestors also wore them to spell out a messages. In the past, it was common for rings to be given that spelled out a word with the first letter of each gemstone. The word "regard," for instance, could be read in a ring containing ruby, emerald, garnet, amethyst, ruby, and diamond.

In the final analysis, you should wear gemstones of any sort when you feel the need for them. If they are beautiful and can be openly worn as decorations, so much the better.

magic squares

PEOPLE HAVE BEEN fascinated with magic squares (called *yantras* in India) for thousands of years. A magic square is a series of numbers arranged in the form of a square in which each horizontal, vertical, and diagonal row adds up to the same total. Some magic squares have as many as forty different ways of reaching this total. Mathematicians find them satisfying from a mathematical point of view, and many people, such as Benjamin Franklin, have spent countless hours constructing magic squares and devising new formulas for creating them. Their mathematical perfection made them a natural addition to amulets and talismans.

History

Magic squares are extremely old and are believed to have originally come from China.[1] The Chinese have a legend that tells how Wu of Hsia found the first magic square in the markings on the shell of a tortoise. He summoned all the wise men of the day to study this phenomenon. From this first magic square came feng shui, Chinese astrology, and numerology. Magic squares spread from China to Japan and southeast Asia and then on to India, Arabia, and Europe. The earliest written reference to magic squares in the West can be found in the writings of Theon of Smyrna, which date back to about 130 C.E.[2] The earliest Arabian reference to magic squares dates back to the ninth century, when Tâbit ibn Quorra wrote on the subject. In early Hebrew Cabalistic writings, the three-by-three magic square represented the forbidden name of God.

Talismanic magic squares came into their own in the fifteenth and sixteenth centuries. Abramelin the Mage, who lived on the banks of the Nile in the fifteenth century, wrote a comprehensive course on ceremonial magic for his son, Lamech. It made extensive use of magic squares and enabled the person who followed the system to attain anything he or she desired. Aleister Crowley, the well-known twentieth-century ceremonial magician, author, researcher, and self-proclaimed "Great Beast," is believed to have gained much of his knowledge as a result of studying this particular system.

The early-sixteenth-century magus Cornelius Agrippa had a major influence on the art of talisman magic. He spent a great deal of time studying a series of magic squares that he named after the planets.

Dr. John Dee, astrologer to Queen Elizabeth I, and Edward Kelley produced the Angelic Tablets, which were magic squares that were used four centuries later in the Enochian system used by the Esoteric Order of the Golden Dawn.

Paul Carus, the eminent occultist, considered magic squares to be "conspicuous instances of the intrinsic harmony of number. . . . There is no science that teaches the harmonies of nature more clearly than mathematics, and the magic squares are like a mirror which reflects the symmetry of the divine norm immanent in all things."[3]

Each magic square is related to the Cabalistic Tree of Life. The Tree of Life was devised to help initiates understand the nature of the powers that he or she would be using. It consists of ten *sephiroth*, or attributes, that depict everything in life. They are:

- Kether–Crown
- Chokmah–Wisdom
- Binah–Understanding
- Chesed–Mercy
- Gevurah–Severity
- Tiphareth–Beauty
- Netsach–Victory

- Hod–Splendor
- Yesod–Foundation
- Malkuth–Kingdom

Each sephira has a number of associations, ranging from angels, intelligences, planets, elements, and magic squares. The magic square of Saturn, for instance, is a three-by-three magic square because Saturn corresponds to Binah, the third sephirah in the Tree of Life. Likewise, as Mercury corresponds to Hod, the eighth sephirah, it is an eight-by-eight magic square.

Magic squares can be used on their own as complete talismans for particular purposes. However, they are more usually used to provide additional power to a talisman or to create seals and sigils (which I'll cover later).

Yantras

Yantras are Indian magic squares and are a form of *mandala*. Mandalas are circular designs drawn around a central point that symbolizes the universe. They are usually constructed for meditation purposes, and the act of drawing them is as important as the later meditation. In India both pictorial yantras and magic square yantras are common, but it's the magic square yantra that is frequently used as a talisman. There are two types of magic square yantras: astrological and personal.

ASTROLOGICAL YANTRAS

You might choose to construct an astrological yantra when you require additional energy from any of the planets. The most common reason for this is when a particular planet is afflicted in someone's natal chart. Astrological yantras use the same magic squares that are found in Western talismanic magic. The original Saturn square came from China. However, these squares have been found in Sanskrit, Tibetan, Arabic, Persian, Greek, and Hebrew alphabets, showing how quickly this knowledge spread around the world.[4]

Ideally, yantras should be made at the correct time according to the planetary hours (see page 97). However, they can be constructed at any time if the need is urgent, or you are making a temporary yantra. Some people scratch yantras into the ground and use them for meditation purposes. Yantras of this sort can be made at any time. Talismanic yantras are usually drawn on paper or engraved on metal. The first yantra I saw was on a filthy scrap of paper that a New Delhi rickshaw driver carried in a small pouch around his neck. Whenever possible, I prefer to use a sheet of good-quality paper that has not previously been used for any other purpose.

Saturn yantra

The Saturn yantra enhances opportunities for achieving worldly success and can also help cure depression.

Naturally, it is also used to rectify problems caused by an afflicted Saturn in the natal chart.

4	9	2
3	5	7
8	1	6

Jupiter yantra

The Jupiter yantra gives the wearer power, prestige, authority, and confidence. It also rectifies problems caused by an afflicted Jupiter in the natal chart.

1	15	14	4
12	6	7	9
8	10	11	5
13	3	2	16

Mars yantra

The Mars yantra protects the wearer from accidents and injury. This five-by-five magic square also rectifies difficulties caused by an afflicted Mars in the natal chart.

11	24	7	20	3
4	12	25	8	16
17	5	13	21	9
10	18	1	14	22
23	6	19	2	15

Sun yantra

The sun yantra is constructed to rectify the negative aspects of an afflicted sun and also to provide peace of mind. Each row of the sun yantra adds up to 111, and the sum of all the numbers is 666.

3	32	3	34	35	1
7	11	27	28	8	30
19	14	16	15	23	24
18	20	22	21	17	13
25	29	10	9	26	12
36	5	33	4	2	31

Venus yantra

The Venus yantra is a popular one as it makes one more attractive to the opposite sex. It also enhances peace of mind and rectifies problems caused by an afflicted Venus in the natal chart.

22	47	16	41	10	35	4
5	23	48	17	42	11	29
30	6	24	49	18	36	12
13	31	7	25	43	19	37
38	14	32	1	26	44	20
21	39	8	33	2	27	45
46	15	40	9	34	3	28

Mercury yantra

The Mercury yantra rectifies problems caused when this planet is afflicted in the natal chart. It also provides protection against enemies and can increase your memory retention.

8	58	59	5	4	62	63	1
49	15	14	52	53	11	10	56
41	23	22	44	45	19	18	48
32	34	35	29	28	38	39	25
40	26	27	37	36	30	31	33
17	47	46	20	21	43	42	24
9	55	54	12	13	51	50	16
64	2	3	61	60	6	7	57

Moon yantra

The Moon yantra rectifies problems created by an afflicted Moon in the natal chart and also provides good friends and respect in the community. Each row adds up to 369, and the sum of all the numbers is 3,321.

37	78	29	70	21	62	13	54	5
6	38	79	30	71	22	63	14	46
47	7	39	80	31	72	23	55	15
16	48	8	40	81	32	64	24	56
57	17	49	9	41	73	33	65	25
26	58	18	50	1	42	74	34	66

67	27	59	10	51	2	43	75	35
36	68	19	60	11	52	3	44	76
77	28	69	20	61	12	54	4	45

NAV-GRAHA YANTRAS

Nav-Graha yantras are another kind of astrological yantra. We have already discussed the Nav-Ratna gem-stones in the previous chapter. Here are the nine magic squares that accompany them. They are intended to be used only to ward off the negative aspects of afflicted planets in the natal horoscope. They should be written on paper and carried in a purse or wallet. Alternatively, they can be carried in a small pouch hung around the neck.

The Nav-Graha squares should be carried for a period of time from forty to forty-three days, starting on a day that is propitious for the planet concerned.

Sun

6	1	8
7	5	3
2	9	4

Moon

7	2	9
8	6	4
3	10	5

Mars

8	3	10
9	7	5
4	11	6

Mercury

9	4	11
10	8	6
5	12	7

Jupiter

10	5	12
11	9	7
6	13	8

Venus

11	6	13
12	10	8
7	14	9

Saturn

12	7	14
13	11	9
8	15	10

Rahu

13	8	15
14	12	10
9	16	11

Ketu

14	9	16
15	13	11
10	17	12

PERSONAL YANTRAS

Personal yantras are constructed to increase confidence, self-esteem, and success. They are four-by-four magic squares based on the person's full date of birth. I was born on December 9, 1946, and my personal yantra looks like this:

12	9	46	5
44	7	10	11
6	47	8	11
10	9	8	45

Each horizontal and vertical row adds up to seventy-two, as do the diagonals. Even more remarkable is that the numbers at the four corners of the yantra also total seventy-two, as do the numbers in each quarter of the magic square. In the top left hand quarter we have the numbers twelve, nine, forty-four, and seven. They total seventy-two, as do forty-six, five, ten, and eleven (top right-hand quarter), six, forty-seven, ten, and nine (bottom left-hand quarter) and eight, eleven, eight, and forty-five (bottom right-hand quarter). Naturally, the four numbers in the center of the yantra (seven, ten, forty-seven, and eight) also total seventy-two.

A personal yantra is almost a perfect magic square. A perfect magic square uses each number just once (see the Jupiter yantra on page 162 for an example of a perfect magic square). This is not possible with personal yantras, as the starting point is our complete date of birth.

Although math is not one of my strong points, I still find incredible beauty in personal yantras. It also astonishes me that they are so easy to construct. Virtually no math is required.

The first number to be entered is the month of birth. I was born in December, the twelfth month of the year. Consequently, I put a twelve in the first position.

12	—	—	—
—	—	—	—
—	—	—	—
—	—	—	—

Next to this goes the day of birth, in my case a nine.

12	9	—	—
—	—	—	—
—	—	—	—
—	—	—	—

The third number is the final two digits of the year of birth. I was born in 1946, so place forty-six in the third position.

12	9	46	—
—	—	—	—
—	—	—	—
—	—	—	—

There is one last number to be placed in the top row. This is my Life Path number, which you may remember we discussed earlier (see page 127). It is my month, day and year of birth added together, and then reduced to a single digit (unless, of course, you find a Master number in the reduction process). My Life Path number is a five.

12	9	46	5
—	—	—	—
—	—	—	—
—	—	—	—

This means that I have the numbers twelve, nine, forty-six, and five in the top row of my personal yantra.

The remaining three rows are just as easy. Here is a formula, which does most of the work for you. The square on the right shows letters for each position.

A	B	C	D		A	B	C	D
C-2	D+2	A-2	B+2		E	F	G	H
D+1	C+1	B-1	A-1		I	J	K	L
B+1	A-3	D+3	C-1		M	N	O	P

The best way to learn this is to construct personal yantras for members of your own family. You will find that it is possible to have zeroes and negative numbers in some yantras. People born in January or February, for example, will always have at least one negative number in their yantras. This is because in position N we have A-3. For someone born in January, we will have negative two in this position. There will also be negative one in position G and a zero is position L. This makes no difference to the chart. Imagine you were constructing a chart for someone born on January 1, 1982. We'll assume her name is Cheryl. Cheryl's personal yantra would look like this.

1	1	80	22
78	24	-1	3
23	81	0	0
2	-2	25	79

(Cheryl has twenty-two, a Master number, for her Life Path. As it is a Master number, we do not reduce it to a single digit.)

Cheryl's yantra adds up to 104 in every direction. In the second row we have the following numbers: seventy-eight, twenty-four, negative-one, and three. Seventy-eight added to twenty-four is 102. We then subtract one, as the third number in the row is negative one. This gives us 101. Finally, we add the final number, which is a three, and this gives us a total of 104. Check out the other combinations for yourself, and you will find that despite having two negative numbers and two zeroes in her magic square, Cheryl's personal yantra totals 104 in every combination.

Although personal yantras are usually used as amulets and talismans, they can also be interpreted to provide clues to the person's character.

OTHER PERSONAL YANTRAS

Personal yantras provide protection in all areas of life. However, special yantras can be constructed to attract specific results. The most common of these are love and money. More yantras are also listed in appendix D.

Personal yantras for love

Everyone wants to find a special someone to share his or her life with. Some people have no difficulty finding the right partner, but others spend many years in fruitless searches for the right person. A love yantra acts as a talisman to attract the right person to you.

Before constructing a love yantra, you need to decide exactly what you want. Are you looking for a partner to share your life with? Do you want a partner who will ultimately be the mother or father of your children? Or are you looking for something altogether different?

In numerology, the number two relates to close relationships. Number six relates to home and family. (The chart on page 127 shows other correspondences.) We will start by constructing a yantra that relates to number two.

You may remember that the first row of my personal yantra was

12   9   46   5

These numbers add up to seventy-two, and

$$7 + 2 = 9.$$

Naturally, I cannot change my month, day, or year of birth. However, I can change the final number to make the first row of the yantra total any number I wish. To create a yantra that would attract love to me, all I need do is change the final number so that when all four numbers are added up, the total can be reduced down to a two. In my case, I would have to change the five to a seven. This gives me

$$12 + 9 + 46 + 7 = 74$$

and then

$$7 + 4 = 11.$$

In this case, we reduce again

$$1 + 1 = 2.$$

(As eleven is a Master number, I would not normally reduce it down to a single digit but would keep it as an eleven, which is, in effect, a "super" two.)

I can now create a yantra square to attract love using the same formula described on page 170.

12	9	46	7
44	9	10	11
8	47	8	11
10	9	10	45

The best times to draw a love yantra are from the tenth through the twentieth of any month. Once your personal love yantra has been constructed, you need to keep it in your purse or wallet until the right person comes into your life. Take it out and look at it for at least sixty seconds every day. Picture your ideal person in your mind as you stare at the yantra. You do not need to actually see this person. All you need obtain is an impression of some of this person's character traits and how you feel when you are with him or her. Once you have done this, replace the yantra in your purse or wallet and carry on with your day, confident that you are attracting your ideal partner to you.

Here is the love yantra I would construct for myself if I were looking for both a partner and a family.

12	9	46	2
44	4	10	11
3	47	8	11
10	9	5	45

As you can see, I have subtracted three from my Life Path number of five, as this means the magic square can be reduced down to a six like so.

$$12 + 9 + 46 + 2 = 69$$

$$6 + 9 = 15$$

$$1 + 5 = 6.$$

There is also a standard yantra magic square to attract love and friendship. This is intended to attract more people into your life, rather than a specific individual. It is used in the same way as the other yantras, and should be kept with you at all times. It should be drawn up on a Friday.

4	15	10	5
14	1	8	11
7	12	13	2
9	6	3	16

Personal yantras for wealth

It would be hard to find anyone who wouldn't like more money. Even extremely wealthy people usually would like just a little bit more. A money yantra acts as a talisman that will attract money to you. In numerology, the number eight is the number of money and finance. Consequently, to attract more money into our lives, we need to construct a magic square in which each row reduces down to an eight.

Each row of my personal yantra reduces down to a nine. As I want my money yantra to reduce down to eight, all I have to do is subtract one from my Life Path number of five, replacing the final number in the top row with a four. (In actuality, I could place any number in this position that reduced down to a four. Consequently, thirteen, twenty-two, thirty-one, forty—even 1,003—could be used, if desired. In practice, I either add or subtract to reach the closest number that enables me to create the magic square.) Here is my money yantra.

12	9	46	4
44	6	10	11
5	47	8	11
10	9	7	45

The best time to draw up a money yantra is on any Thursday or Friday morning that falls from the first through tenth days of any month. The money yantra is used in the same way as the yantras for love. It should be kept close to you at all times. At least once a day, you should stare at it for sixty seconds while thinking how much better your life will be once you have more money. You might request a specific amount of money. If you do this, aim high. As life generally gives us what we ask for, be bold and ask for a large amount. I normally ask for whatever it is I want, rather than request money directly. The important thing is to have a specific amount of money or a specific object in mind while you stare at the yantra. After sixty seconds, put the yantra away and carry on with whatever it is you are doing.

Seals and Sigils

There are two notable ways to conceal and personalize magic squares and yantras: magical seals and sigils.

MAGICAL SEALS

A magical seal is a geometric design made by lines created when every number in a magic square is touched in numerical order. Some of these designs are astonishingly beautiful (Mercury, for instance). Seals contain the essence of the magic squares and can be used instead of them when desired. A magical seal is frequently used in preference to a magic square when secrecy or confidentiality is required. If I wanted to carry a specific talisman around with me, and felt that it might be seen by others, I would probably use a seal, rather than a magic square.

SIGILS

A sigil is a signature that personalizes a magic square even further. Traditionally, the Hebrew name of the magic square's protective angel was turned into numbers, using a special chart known as the Aiq Beker. These numbers were then connected by lines on the magic square to create a sigil, or signature. Many people still use this method today. However, unless you speak and read Hebrew, the chances of making mistakes are extremely high.

For most people, it makes more sense to create a sigil using the Pythagorean system of numerology. It is simple and straightforward with little chance of error. You can create a sigil using any word you wish. For talismanic purposes, it is best to create a sigil using either your own first name or the name of the planetary angel connected with the particular square (see appendix A).

Here is a simple Pythagorean chart to help turn your name into numbers.

1	2	3	4	5	6	7	8	9
A	B	C	D	E	F	G	H	I
J	K	L	M	N	O	P	Q	R
S	T	U	V	W	X	Y	Z	

My first name is Richard. This converts to 9938194 as R = 9, I = 9, C = 3, H = 8, A = 1, R = 9, and D = 4. If I wanted, for example, to grow spiritually and philosophically, I could create a magic square of Jupiter and then join up the numbers in my first name, creating a personal sigil that would add additional power to the magic square. I start this by drawing a small circle inside the first box in the second row of the Jupiter magic square (see page 162). This contains the number nine, which relates to *R* in Richard (according to the Pythagorean chart above). *I*, the second letter in Richard, also relates to the number nine, so I don't do anything for that letter. The *C* in Richard relates to number three, so next I draw a straight line from the small circle in the nine box to the center of the box containing the number three (third position on the bottom row). From this box, I now draw a straight line to the eight box, because this relates to the *H* in Richard. I continue connecting numbers with lines until I have connected all the numbers in my name. This creates the Jupiter sigil for Richard.

If I wanted to, I could even eliminate the magic square, and carry the sigil with me as a talisman. This would be advantageous because no one except me would know what it was.

Letter Magic Squares

Magic squares comprised of letters rather than numbers come from the Latin tradition. One of the most famous of these is the Sator Arepo magic square, which can be found in mosaics in a number of Roman sites, including Cirencester in England and Pompeii. The exact meaning of the words "sator arepo" has been disputed, but it is generally considered to read: "Sator, the sower, holds the wheels by his work."[5] It is still frequently used as a protective talisman (and also as an amulet to protect the wearer from the evil eye).

S	A	T	O	R
A	R	E	P	O
T	E	N	E	T
O	P	E	R	A
R	O	T	A	S

Several letter squares can be found in *The Book of the Sacred Magic of Abramelin the Mage*,[6] including a slightly different version of the Sator Arepo square, which is in-tended to be used to win the love of a maiden:

S	A	L	O	M
A	R	E	P	O
L	E	M	E	L
O	P	E	R	A
M	O	L	A	S

Here is another example from Abramelin, which is in-tended to make a spirit appear in human form.

L	E	V	I	A	T	A	N
E	R	M	O	G	A	S	A
V	M	I	R	T	E	A	T
I	O	R	A	N	T	G	A
A	G	T	N	A	R	O	I
T	A	E	T	R	I	M	V
A	S	A	G	O	M	R	E
N	A	T	A	I	V	E	L

None of the squares mentioned by Abramelin are in-tended to be used on their own, and will not work unless you follow his six-month preparation period first. I know a number of people who have attempted this pro-gram, but it is arduous, and a huge amount of dedication is required. I do not know anyone who has succeeded.

Here is a traditional letter square that helps unlock the door to the future.

M	I	L	O	N
I	R	A	G	O
L	A	M	A	L
O	G	A	R	I
N	O	L	I	M

Other Letter Talismans

People have experimented with different types of letter talismans for thousands of years, and this research is still ongoing today.

ALPHABETIC SIGILS

The turn-of-the-century British surrealist artist A. O. Spare devised a simple yet highly effective system that he called "alphabetic sigils."

To create one, you need to think of a worthwhile goal or desire. You must be as specific as possible. It is not enough to say, for example, "I want more money." You need to state the exact amount and the date you want to have it in your possession. Instead, you might say, "I want to have five thousand dollars by August tenth."

Before you proceed with creating the sigil, take some time to confirm that your original request is accurate. Think about your desire at odd times; visualize what your life will be like once you have it. Meditate on it. You might, for example, decide that five thousand dollars is not enough, or perhaps you need it a month or two earlier. After you've slept on the matter, you can go through your request sentence again and make any necessary changes. You might, for example, change your request so that it now reads:

"I want to have seven thousand dollars by July fourth."

Write the sentence on a piece of paper, making sure to write out any numbers or symbols. For the next step, we go through a process of elimination. The first word of your request is *I*. Go through the sentence, and see if it contains any further *I*s. There are none, so you next look at the second letter, which is *W*. Again, go through the sentence and delete any other *W*s. Again there are none. It is a different matter with the third letter, though. This is the letter *A*. There are *A*s in the words "have," "thousand," and "dollars." Strike these letters out. The sentence now reads:

"I want to hve seven thousnd dollrs by July fourth"

Repeat with all of the letters, until you end up with each letter being used only once. The process, in this example, goes as follows.

I want to have seven thousand dollars by July fourth
I want to hve seven thousnd dollrs by July fourth
(eliminating additional *A*s.)
I want to have seve thousd dollrs by July fourth
(eliminating additional *N*s.)
I want o hve seve housd dollrs by July fourh
(eliminating additional *T*s.)
I want o hve seve husd dllrs by July furh
(eliminating additional *O*s.)
I want o hve seve usd dllrs by July fur
(eliminating additional *H*s.)
I want o hve see usd dllrs by July fur
(eliminating additional *V*s.)
I want o hve s usd dllrs by July fur
(eliminating additional *E*s)
I want o hve s ud dllr by July fur
(eliminating additional *S*s.)
I want o hve s ud dllr by Jly fr
(Eliminating additional *U*s)
I want o hve s ud llr by Jly fr
(Eliminating additional *D*s.)
I want o hve s ud lr by Jy fr
(Eliminating additional *L*s.)
I want o hve s ud lr by Jy fr
(Eliminating additional *R*s.)
I want o hve s ud lr by J f
(Eliminating additional *B*s. There are none, so we elimi-
nate any duplicates of the next letter, *Y*.)

There are no duplicates of the remaining letters (*J* or *F*), so our talismanic message is now complete.

Write this message on a piece of vellum, eliminating any spaces between the words. It makes no difference if you write the message in capital or small letters. Here is what the example message looks like.

iwantohvesudlrbyjf

Every time you look at this message, you will know exactly what it means, but it will be incomprehensible to anyone else. When I do this, I further disguise the original words by arranging the letters in groups of three. This means that the example talisman would look like this:

iwa nto hve sud lrb yjf

You might prefer to have the letters in a long line, split them up into random groups, or write them out in reverse order. A friend of mine signs his requests with his first name, which is then included in the reduction process. He feels that this makes him an intrinsic part of the process. It makes no difference what you do with the letters, just as long as the message is instantly recognizable to you, whenever you see it.

Mr. Spare suggested that you concentrate on this alphabetical sigil for a few seconds and then forget about it, trusting that the universe will produce your desire for you. I prefer to look at the talisman for a few seconds two or three times a day. Every time I see it, I consciously send my request out into the universe.

final thoughts

TALISMANS, AMULETS, AND lucky charms have played a valuable, and largely hidden, role in the evolution of mankind. The number of people they have helped is incalculable. Although some people feel that they are part of our past, they still have an important role to play, today, and in the future. How many people would walk past a four-leaf clover without picking it up? How many people have a "lucky" coin or other object which they carry around with them? Just the other day I spoke to a professional speaker who would not go out on stage without his lucky handkerchief. As long as people feel the need for good luck, protection, or assistance in attaining a goal, magical objects will be in demand.

Knowledge and expertise in these areas gives you more power and control over your life. You will find you have more confidence in your abilities when you use charms, amulets, and talismans. Use them wisely and your progress through life will become easier because you will be utilizing and harnessing the universal forces to attract to you what you want, and to repel and deter anything you do not want.

One of the things I especially like about magical objects such as these is that they give me plenty of freedom. I can use my own taste to purchase suitable charms and amulets, and I can use my own creativity to draw up a talisman that reflects my personal needs and desires. Something that I choose for a charm may not appeal to you, but it will be right for me. Likewise, an amulet that you wear may not appeal to me, but will perform its protective task perfectly for you. Our own individuality is reflected at every stage.

Not everyone feels this way, though, and you are bound to come across people who tell you that talismans have to be made in the same style as that used by medieval magicians. If they believe that, these are obviously the correct talismans for them, but they may not be so for you. You are your own person. Use your imagination, sense of beauty, and all of your creativity to find and design magical that will be perfect for you.

Talismans, amulets, and lucky charms give you an edge in the world we live in. Because of this, they must be used responsibly and ethically. If you use them only for good, they will look after you and make your life fuller, more satisfying, and much more rewarding.

appendix

planetary & zodiacal tables

Planetary Correspondences

SUN

> **Zodiac sign:** Leo
>
> **Color:** yellow, orange, gold
>
> **Metal:** gold
>
> **Gemstone/Mineral:** topaz, diamond
>
> **Tree:** oak
>
> **Element:** fire
>
> **Angel:** Michael (Some authorities say that Raphael
> looks after the interests of the sun.)

The sun is associated with activity, leadership, authority, self-expression, fame, strength, masculinity, men's mysteries, business activities, career advancement, and success. The hours and days of the sun are good times to start new projects.

MOON

Zodiac sign: Cancer

Color: white, cream, silver

Metal: Silver

Gemstone/Mineral: moonstone, pearl, opal

Tree: walnut

Element: water

Angel: Gabriel

The moon is associated with intuition, instinct, emotions, sensitivity, the subconscious, cycles, rhythms, fertility, children, femininity, women's mysteries, the home, and anything to do with water, such as overseas travel, navigation, and maritime trade. The hours and days of the moon are good times for divinations.

MERCURY

Zodiac signs: Gemini and Virgo

Color: yellow, orange, purple

Metal: Mercury (quicksilver) and zinc (use silver when making talismans)

Gemstone/Mineral: agate, opal, citrine

Tree: olive

Element: air

Angel: Raphael (Some authorities claim that
Michael looks after the interests of Mercury.)

Mercury is associated with the intellect, thought, analysis, education, mathematics, science, versatility, communication, self-expression, travel, trade, commerce, and healing. The hours and days of Mercury are good times for learning and communicating with others.

VENUS

Zodiac signs: Taurus and Libra

Color: green, pink

Metal: copper

Gemstone/Mineral: emerald, turquoise

Tree: myrtle

Element: air

Angel: Aniel

Venus is associated with beauty, creativity, compassion, love, friendship, personal and business partnerships, co-operation, fashion, the arts, recreation, good taste, aesthetic qualities, and financial well-being. The hours and days of Venus are good times for matters involving love and friendship.

MARS

Zodiac signs: Aries and Scorpio

Color: strong, vibrant reds

Metal: iron, steel

Gemstone/Mineral: ruby, bloodstone, garnet

Tree: holly

Element: fire

Angel: Camael

Mars is associated with drive, determination, competitiveness, athletic activities, courage, legal matters, the armed forces, confrontation, aggression, wars, engineering, and sharp objects. The hours and days of Mars are good times for working on obstacles and difficulties.

JUPITER

Zodiac signs: Sagittarius and Pisces

Color: Blue, purple

Metal: tin

Gemstone/Mineral: amethyst, sapphire

Tree: birch

Element: fire

Angel: Zadkiel

Jupiter is associated with expansion, growth, financial matters, prosperity, wisdom, dignity, moral values, education, religion, spirituality, philosophy, good judgment, and long trips. The hours and days of Jupiter are good times for working on anything to do with expansion and ultimate success.

SATURN

    Zodiac signs: Capricorn and Aquarius

    Color: black, gray, dark brown

    Metal: lead, pewter

    Gemstone/Mineral: obsidian, jet, smoky quartz

    Tree: yew

    Element: earth

    Angel: Zaphiel

Saturn is associated with frustrations, limitations, restrictions, perseverance, experience, maturity, death, karma, destiny, agriculture, real estate, morality, responsibilities, and status. The hours and days of Saturn are good for practical matters that need to be attended to.

Zodiacal Correspondences

ARIES / FIRST HOUSE

Glyph: ♈

Planet: Mars

Symbol: ram

Element: fire

Gems: bloodstone, fire agate, diamond

Day: Tuesday

Color: scarlet, red

Metal: iron

Angels: Camael, Sammael, Zamael

Arians are enthusiastic, quick-witted, and natural leaders. They want to be first, and because of this, they often rush in before thinking about the situation first.

Aries rules the first house. This relates to the person making the talisman, and his or her physical body, ego, personality, temperament, health, and goals or aspirations.

TAURUS / SECOND HOUSE

Glyph: ♉

Planet: Venus

Symbol: bull

Element: earth

Gems: emerald, lapis lazuli, malachite, turquoise

Day: Friday

Color: pink

Metal: copper

Angels: Anael, Aniel, Araziel, Asimodel

Taureans are persistent, patient, reliable, stable, and careful. They enjoy the pleasures and comforts that money can provide. They are frequently interested in aesthetic and creative pursuits and do well if they can channel these interests into a career.

Taurus rules the second house, and this relates to earning ability, money matters, investments and possessions.

GEMINI / THIRD HOUSE

Glyph: ♊

Planet: Mercury

Symbol: twins

Element: air

Gems: agate, amber, yellow citrine, pearl, topaz

Day: Wednesday

Color: yellow

Metal: quicksilver

Angels: Ambriel, Michael, Saraiel

People born under the sign of Gemini are sympathetic, generous, affectionate, and have restless, active minds. They are good talkers and enjoy stimulating, humorous conversations. Gemini is a twin-bodied sign (the twins), and Geminians often perform two or more activities at the same time.

Gemini rules the third house, which relates to everyday matters, close relationships, and communication. It also relates to short trips.

CANCER / FOURTH HOUSE

Glyph: ♋

Planet: moon

Symbol: crab

Element: water

Gems: chalcedony, moonstone, white opal, ruby, white serpentine

Day: Monday

Color: white, silver

Metal: silver, white gold and platinum

Angels: Abuzhar, Muriel, Phakiel

Cancerians are generally reserved, sensitive, and changeable. They are influenced by the events and people around them and are easily hurt by others. They retain a strong love of home and family.

Cancer rules the fourth house, which relates to real estate, including the family home. It also relates to personal and private matters, as well as endings of all sorts.

LEO / FIFTH HOUSE

Glyph: ♌

Planet: sun

Symbol: Lion

Element: fire

Gems: red carnelian, citrine, peridot, sardonyx,
   sun stone

Day: Sunday

Color: orange, gold

Metal: gold

Angels: Raphael, Seratiel, Verchiel

Leos are ambitious, independent, outspoken, and usually
happy people. They enjoy being the center of attention
and like being recognized and admired by others.

Leo rules the fifth house, which relates to love, romance, children, pleasures, athletics, hobbies, and creative activities.

VIRGO

Glyph: ♍

Planet: Mercury

Symbol: virgin

Element: earth

Gems: sapphire, tourmaline

Day: Friday

Color: pale yellows and blues

Metal: alloys

Angels: Hamaliel, Michael, Schaltiel

Virgos are modest, serious, hard-working, health conscious, and thoughtful. They enjoy system and order, and prefer the details to the overall picture.

Virgo rules the sixth house, which relates to work, career, health, and service to others. It also relates to pets and other animals.

LIBRA / SEVENTH HOUSE

Glyph: ♎

Planet: Venus

Symbol: scales

Element: air

Gems: aquamarine, quartz, opal, sapphire

Day: Wednesday

Color: pale blue, pink, gray

Metal: copper

Angels: Abael, Aniel, Chadakiel, Haniel, Zuriel

Librans are peace-loving, harmonious, agreeable people who make an effort to get along well with others. They are natural peacemakers and enjoying restoring balance to difficult situations.

Libra rules the seventh house, which relates to matters involving positive and negative partnerships, both business and personal. It also relates to enemies.

SCORPIO / EIGHTH HOUSE

Glyph: ♏

Planet: Mars or Pluto

Symbol: scorpion

Element: water

Gems: obsidian, opal, topaz, black tourmaline

Day: Saturday

Color: dark red

Metal: lead

Angels: Barbiel, Barchiel, Camael, Sammael, Sartzeil, Zamael

Scorpios are shrewd, critical, tenacious, secretive, and determined. They possess ambition and drive and usually achieve their goals.

Scorpio rule the eighth house, which relates to endings and problems of all sorts. It also relates to the occult, sex, taxes, surgery, and other people's money.

SAGITTARIUS / NINTH HOUSE

Glyph: ♐

Planet: Jupiter

Symbol: archer

Element: fire

Gems: purple fluorite, magnetite, turquoise

Day: Thursday

Color: purple, green

Metal: tin

Angels: Adnachiel, Advachiel, Bethor, Saritiel, Zachariel, Zadkiel

Sagittarians are cheerful, positive, generous, and independent. They are mentally (and sometimes physically) active and always need something exciting to look forward to. Despite frequently finding themselves in trouble by saying exactly what they think, Sagittarians usually manage to get what they want.

Sagittarius rules the ninth house, which relates to philosophy, religions, science, higher learning, and distant travel. It is also concerned with dreams and visions.

CAPRICORN / TENTH HOUSE

Glyph: ♑

Planet: Saturn

Symbol: goat

Element: earth

Gems: azurite, garnet, indicolite, tourmaline

Day: Saturday

Color: black, brown

Metal: lead

Angels: Aratron, Kafziel, Orifiel, Semaqiel

Capricornians are serious, thoughtful, practical people. They are determined and possess enormous perseverance. They normally achieve success late in life, as they are tenacious and never give up on their goals. Capricornians often look older than their years when they are young but reverse this and look younger than their years when they grow old.

Capricorn rules the tenth house, which represents your reputation and standing in the community. It is also related to self-esteem, recognition, and authority figures.

AQUARIUS / ELEVENTH HOUSE

Glyph: ♒

Planet: Saturn or Uranus

Symbol: water carrier

Element: air

Gems: amethyst, diamond, opal

Day: Saturday

Color: blue, white

Metal: lead

Angels: Cambiel, Gambiel, Kafziel, Orifiel, Tzak-maqiel, Zaphiel

Aquarians are tolerant, generous humanitarians. They are more concerned with humanity in general than with individuals. Consequently, they can appear slightly detached. They generally have a strong interest in psychic and occult subjects.

Aquarius rules the eleventh house, which relates to humanitarian activities and relationships with others. It also relates to circumstances that are out of our control, hopes and dreams, and love received from others.

PISCES / TWELFTH HOUSE

Glyph: ✵

Planet: Jupiter or Neptune

Symbol: two fish

Element: water

Gems: bloodstone, coral, mother of pearl, pearl

Day: Thursday

Color: royal blue, purple, green

Metal: tin

Angels: Barakiel, Barchiel, Vocatiel, Zachariel, Zadkiel

Pisceans are honest, caring, emotional, and kind. They enjoy neatness and order and sometimes have difficulty in making decisions.

Pisces rules the twelfth house, which relates to mental health, secrets, the subconscious mind, karmic debts, limitations, and restrictions. It also relates to latent talents and hidden strengths.

Groupings of the Twelve Houses

The houses can be grouped in a number of ways, but possibly the most useful division for constructing talismans is to divide them by the elements of fire, earth, air, and water. When you decide to use a particular house in a talisman, it pays to look at the qualities of the other houses in the same group, as they may add strength and power to your talisman.

FIRE

The fire houses relate to the person him- or herself. Fire is spontaneous, energetic, enthusiastic, and romantic.

First house: Aries, the physical body

Fifth house: Leo, the soul

Ninth house: Sagittarius, the mind

EARTH

The earth houses relate to home, family, and community. Earth is concerned with material comforts, sensuality, and practicality.

Second house: Taurus, possessions

Sixth house: Virgo, work, career

Tenth house: Capricorn, recognition

AIR

The air houses are concerned with the other people in our lives. Air enjoys communicating and is logical, idealistic, and broad-minded.

Third house: Gemini, unchosen relationships, such as relatives and neighbors.

Seventh house: Libra, one-to-one relationships, such as friends and lovers.

Eleventh house: Aquarius, wider friendships, such as members of the same organization or club.

WATER

The water houses are concerned with endings. Water is emotional, intuitive, and easily influenced by the moods and desires of others.

Fourth house: Cancer, death of the physical body

Eight house: Scorpio, release of the soul

Twelfth house: Pisces, karma

appendix

the seven famous talismans

THE TALISMAN OF THE SUN

This talisman should be made on a Sunday, while the moon is passing through the first ten degrees of Leo and is in favorable aspect to both the sun and Saturn.

A circle enclosed by a pentagram is engraved on one side of a disk of good-quality gold. On the other side, a six-pointed Star of Solomon is engraved with a human head inscribed in its center. Surrounding this is the name of the angel Michael, inscribed in either Hebrew or a magical alphabet (see appendix E).

The talisman of the sun ensures that its owner receives goodwill from influential people. It also protects him or her from a variety of ailments that might otherwise prove fatal.

THE TALISMAN OF THE MOON

The talisman of the moon has to be made on a Monday, while the moon is passing through the first ten degrees of either Capricorn or Virgo and is well aspected to Saturn.

A crescent shape inside a pentagram is engraved on one side of a disk of pure silver. On the other side, a chalice encircled by the Seal of Solomon is engraved. This is surrounded by the name of the angel Gabriel in either Hebrew or a magic alphabet (see appendix E).

The talisman of the moon protects all travelers. It also wards off the possibility of a violent death, as well as death by drowning, epilepsy, dropsy (edema), apoplexy, and madness.

THE TALISMAN OF MARS

The talisman of Mars is made on a Tuesday, while the moon is passing through the first ten degrees of Aries or Sagittarius and is well aspected to Mars and Saturn.

A sword inside a pentagram is engraved on one side of a disk of good-quality iron. A lion's head inside a six-pointed star is engraved on the other side. Around this are letters spelling out the name of the angel Camael in Hebrew or a magical alphabet (see appendix E).

The talisman of Mars protects the wearer from his or her enemies and counteracts negative aspects in the person's horoscope, particularly regarding violent death. It also protects the wearer from the possibility of death in a fight or battle, and it wards off ulcers, fevers, and plagues.

THE TALISMAN OF MERCURY

The talisman of Mercury is made on a Wednesday while the moon is passing through the first ten degrees of Gemini or Scorpio and is well aspected to Mercury and Saturn.

The talisman is engraved on a circle made from an amalgam of silver, mercury, and pewter. A pentagram is engraved on one side. Inside the pentagram is a winged caduceus with two serpents twining around it. On the other side is the Seal of Solomon with a dog's head inside it. Surrounding this was the name of Raphael, written in either Hebrew or a magical alphabet (see appendix E).

The talisman of Mercury is used to attract business and prosperity. It protects the wearer from the schemes and deviousness of others and causes prophetic dreams when worn on the head at night.

THE TALISMAN OF JUPITER

The talisman of Jupiter is made on a Thursday while the moon is passing through the first ten degrees of Libra and is in favorable aspect to Jupiter and Saturn.

A four-pointed crown inside a pentagram is engraved on one side of a disk of pure pewter. A head of an eagle in the center of the Seal of Solomon is engraved on the other. Around this is the name of the angel Zadkiel inscribed in either Hebrew or a magical alphabet (see appendix E).

The talisman of Jupiter makes the wearer appear benevolent, honorable, and sympathetic to others. It attracts and rewards honest endeavors and protects the wearer from unforeseen accidents.

THE TALISMAN OF VENUS

The talisman of Venus should be made on a Friday while the moon is passing through the first ten degrees of Taurus or Virgo and is well aspected to Venus and Saturn.

On one side of a circle of pure copper, the letter G is inscribed in the alphabet of the Magi (see appendix E, page 228). Surrounding this is a pentagram. A six-pointed star with a dove inside it is engraved on the other side. The name of the angel Haniel is engraved in Hebrew or a magical alphabet (see appendix E) around the star.

The talisman of Venus attracts love and harmony and further enhances existing love relationships. It averts spite, malice, and hatred. It also has the power to turn hatred into love. (For this to work, the talisman needs to be dipped into a glass of water, which the person who hates the owner of the talisman must then drink.)

THE TALISMAN OF SATURN

The talisman of Saturn should be made on a Saturday while the moon is passing through the first ten degrees of Taurus or Capricorn and is well aspected to Saturn.

A pentagram enclosing a sickle is inscribed on one side of a circle of lead. The other side shows a bull's head inside a Seal of Solomon. The name of the angel Zaphiel is engraved around this in either Hebrew or a magical alphabet (see appendix E).

The talisman of Saturn protects the wearer from violent death, as well as a variety of illnesses, including consumption, cancer, and dropsy (edema).

appendix

popular birthstones

AGATE

Agate is a variety of quartz that can be found in different colors. Moss agate contains lines and dots that create attractive pictures. The Romans believed that agate was specially blessed because of this quality, and they used all forms of agate for both medicinal and talismanic purposes. It was believed that this stone could avert storms and other natural disasters. In Persia, it was believed to enhance the mind and make the wearer more eloquent. Queen Elizabeth I was presented with a large oval agate as a talisman to ensure she would always have at least one true and faithful friend. Agate makes a highly effective amulet as it both protects and helps provide balance. Agate can also be held in your hands to relieve the effects of constant stress.

AMETHYST

Amethyst was used by the ancients to counteract the effects of too much alcohol. Egyptian soldiers used them as amulets to provide courage and overcome their enemies. The amethyst has also been called "the bishop's stone," and rosaries made from them were believed to eliminate stress and tension. In the Middle Ages, amulets of amethyst were used to ward off business problems and to provide wearers with a sense of calmness when facing difficult situations. Amethyst possesses healing qualities and enhances intuition.

AQUAMARINE AND BERYL

Aquamarine and beryl belong to the same family. Aquamarine ranges in color from white to brilliant blue, while beryl can be found in a variety of greens. In the East, they have always been considered a symbol of purity and are frequently given to brides on their wedding day to strengthen the bonds of love. The Romans also believed that they helped preserve marriages and made the wearer more cheerful and outgoing. They also increased motivation and stimulated the intellect. Aquamarine and beryl were also believed to protect sailors and anyone travelling to distant places. Both provide tranquillity and restore the soul.

BLOODSTONE

Legend says that bloodstone dates from the Crucifixion. After the soldier pierced Jesus with a spear to see if he was still alive, drops of blood fell onto some green jasper on the ground. The blood immediately permeated the stone, creating the first bloodstone. This may be one reason why soldiers carried bloodstone to cauterize wounds.

Bloodstone was worn by the ancient Greeks and Romans to attract favors from important people and to ward off poisonous creatures. Athletes wore it as a talisman for success. Bloodstone stimulates and enhances strength and courage.

CITRINE

The citrine is a member of the quartz family and is used to enhance communication. It also aids thinking and decision-making. Consequently, although it can be worn, it is sometimes better to have a citrine sitting on a table or desk where you work.

DIAMOND

The diamond has always been the most popular stone because of its beauty and power. People were fascinated by the fact that it could cut anything but could not be cut itself. The Romans wore it on their left arms, believing that its touch would make them brave and powerful.[1] Queen Elizabeth I was given a diamond to protect her from the plague, and she wore it in her bosom. Napoleon had the famous Regent diamond mounted in the hilt of his sword. As this stone had brought so much misery and unhappiness to its previous owners, it is surprising that he chose it as a talisman.

Small diamonds are considered more fortunate than large ones, which create anxiety and stress.

EMERALD

The emerald has always been held in high regard because of its brilliant green color. The Romans believed that it could restore failing eyesight. They also believed that emeralds change color when in the presence of falsehood or dishonesty. It is believed to strengthen the memory and provide knowledge of future events. The emerald belongs to Venus, which makes it a gemstone of love. It increases the feelings between two people who really love each other, but it can also break up relationships that are fickle.

GARNET

Garnets have been popular as amulets and talismans for thousands of years, and many examples of engraved garnets can be found in museums around the world. In India and the Middle East, it was commonly worn as an amulet to protect the wearer from lightning, poison, and the plague. In the Middle Ages people wore it to increase their cheerfulness and to make them more attractive to others. It was believed to change color when its owner was in danger.

JADE

Jade is a hard stone that varies in color from white to green. It has always been a popular amulet in Asia, where it is used to protect the wearer from injury and the effects of witchcraft. The Greeks and Romans believed that it protected them from epilepsy, as well as eye, stomach, and kidney problems. Jade is also known as nephrite, which is derived from a Greek word meaning "kidney." Interestingly, when the Spanish explorer Pizzaro conquered Mexico, he found the natives used jade to help treat kidney problems. Sir Walter Raleigh also found that people in Guiana also used jade to help them with stomach and kidney problems.[2] In New Zealand, the native Maori people consider jade to be a sacred heirloom that embodies all the qualities of their ancestors. Consequently, when a man dies his precious jade is passed on to his son. Jade enhances friendship and is said to ensure a long, healthy, worthwhile life.

LAPIS LAZULI

Lapis lazuli is a deep blue, opaque stone that has been used as a talisman for thousands of years. The Egyptians, Greeks, and Romans all created talismans from it. A necklace of lapis lazuli was used to make timid children more confident. It was also considered to relieve melancholy, ensure good friendships, and bring success in love. Lapis lazuli encourages spiritual awareness, honesty, and the growth of wisdom.

MALACHITE

Malachite was used as an amulet in the East to ward off rheumatism. The Romans believed that it would ensure a sound sleep, while at the same time attracting good health, a stable relationship, and financial success. In the Middle Ages it was usually engraved with a symbol of the sun to ensure good health and a positive attitude toward life. Malachite soothes and calms and helps create inner peace and contentment.

MOONSTONE

The moonstone is a form of feldspar. It is related to the moon because its gentle blue color reminded people of moonlight. Moonstone helps reconcile lovers and ensures good fortune in love. It is worn to protect the wearer when traveling and helps promote good health.

ONYX

Onyx, black onyx in particular, is believed to enhance one's faith. Consequently, it has always been a popular stone for rosaries. It is also believed to curtail passion and prevent fits and seizures.

OPAL

Opal is a type of soft quartz that has been revered for thousands of years because it displays all the colors of the rainbow. Opals are sensitive to atmospheric conditions, and reveal their best colors when they are warm, dry, and worn by their owners. In ancient Greece, people believed that opals provided foresight, as long as this talent was not used for personal gain. In the fourteenth century, the opal was used as a talisman to strengthen eyesight and as an amulet to avert the evil eye. Although Sir Walter Scott considered the opal to be a negative stone in his novel *Anne of Geierstein*, the opal is a highly positive and sensitive stone that encourages intuitive insights.

PEARL

The pearl is the only gem that comes from a living organism. Pearls are emblems of femininity and purity. Because pearls resemble tears, they were at one time considered unfortunate for people in love. Some people still believe that today. People who worked with the sea wore pearls as an amulet to protect them from sharks. The pearl restores harmony and encourages the wearer to overcome opposition and create the life he or she has dreamed of living.

PERIDOT

The word "peridot" means "precious stone" in Arabic, and, at one time, it was considered more valuable than the diamond. The Romans wore them as amulets to protect them from melancholy and enchantment. In the Middle Ages, they were worn to provide foreknowledge of future events. Peridot wards off jealousy, negativity, and depression.

RUBY

The ruby has always been considered the most important and powerful stone. It was worn in the East as a talisman that granted health, happiness, and longevity. The Chaldeans thought that it protected them from evil. The Romans believed that it dispelled evil thoughts and promoted justice, honesty, and fair play. Like the garnet, the ruby was believed to change color at the first sign of danger. The ruby symbolizes abundance, success, and eternal love. It energizes both the heart and the soul.

SAPPHIRE

The Buddhists consider sapphire to be the "Stone of Stones" and believe it will grant peace and contentment to its wearers, as long as they lead good, worthwhile lives. The sapphire has always been one of the most prized colored stones. It was believed to preserve chastity and protect the wearer from a variety of illnesses. It also protected the wearer from the effects of black magic.

Emperor Charlemagne's wife had a powerful talisman made from two sapphires and a small piece of the cross of Jesus. It was intended to keep her husband faithful and constant. It did this so effectively that even after she died Charlemagne refused to have his wife buried until his confessor finally removed the talisman from her body.

Sapphire encourages its wearers to dream ambitious dreams and to then achieve them.

SARDONYX

The sardonyx is a reddish-brown stone containing parallel flat bands in red, brown, and white. It has a smooth, hard surface that lends itself to engraving. Because of this, the Romans would carve figures, such as Mars or Hercules, from the top layer, and have them standing in relief against the darker layer underneath. Stones decorated in this way were used as talismans for strength, courage, and fearlessness. The sardonyx was popular because it was believed that it gave the wearer self-control, attracted friends, ensured happiness in conjugal love, and made the person agreeable to others.

TOPAZ

The topaz was called "the stone of strength" by Pliny the Elder and was believed to protect the wearer from the dangers of travel, as well as burns and scalds. In the Middle Ages, it was set in gold and used as an amulet to dispel enchantment. It was also considered to cure asthma and insomnia. Topaz reduces stress and soothes the nerves.

TOURMALINE

Tourmaline was worn as a talisman to attract friends, secure favors, and help provide good ideas. It encourages communication and accord and enables people to discuss difficult subjects in a spirit of cooperation and harmony. It is also the stone of forgiveness and encourages the wearer to forgive him- or herself, as well as others. Consequently, it is sometimes called "the stone of peace."

TURQUOISE

The turquoise has been used in amulets more often than any other stone. This is partly because of its beauty but more because of the mystical qualities it contains. It is believed to attract towards itself any negativity that threatens its owner. In the Middle Ages, people believed that it could prevent headaches, eliminate hatred, and would also change color when its owner was unwell or in danger. The Pueblo of New Mexico considered turquoise a sacred stone, and, at one time, it could only be worn by men. The turquoise symbolizes success and contentment.

ZIRCON

Zircon has been used as a talisman for thousands of years. In India, it is still worn to attract honor, success, wealth, and wisdom. In the Middle Ages, it was believed to stimulate the appetite and aid digestion, as well as protect the wearer from a variety of illnesses.

appendix

additional yantras

YANTRA FOR BUSINESS AND CAREER SUCCESS

This yantra magic square can be used to gain increased business or to achieve a promotion at work. It should be drawn up on any Tuesday and used in the same way as the other yantras.

1	14	11	8
12	7	2	13
6	9	16	3
15	4	5	10

YANTRA FOR OBTAINING WORK

If you are currently out of work or are looking for a new position, this yantra should be drawn up and carried with you until you find work. It can be drawn up at any time.

9	16	5	4
7	2	11	14
12	13	8	1
6	3	10	15

YANTRA FOR FAME AND SUCCESS

This yantra can be used if you want to gain increased recognition in the community or if you want to become famous. It should be drawn up on the first Sunday of any month.

8	4	7	1
6	2	7	5
3	9	2	6
3	5	4	8

YANTRA FOR WEALTH AND ABUNDANCE

This yantra can be used if you want to become rich. It should be drawn up on any Thursday. You should look at it for sixty seconds every morning when you first get up, then again during the day, and again immediately before going to bed.

2	9	2	7
6	3	6	5
8	3	8	1
4	5	4	7

YANTRA FOR RESPECT

This yantra should be constructed and carried with you if you wish to be more respected or held in high regard by others.

56	63	2	7
6	3	60	59
62	57	8	1
4	5	58	61

YANTRA FOR GOOD HEALTH

This yantra should be drawn up and carried whenever you are feeling unwell. It can be constructed at any time.

2	9	2	7
6	3	6	5
8	3	8	1
4	5	4	7

PROTECTIVE YANTRA FOR THE HOME

This yantra eliminates quarrels and discord and also promotes harmony and peace in the home. It should be drawn up in the kitchen of the house on any evening and placed somewhere in the kitchen where it can be seen.

36	29	34
31	33	35
32	37	30

YANTRA TO COUNTERACT THE EVIL EYE

The evil eye is also known in India, and there is a yantra that can be worn to avert and remove the negative effects of the evil eye. You will notice that this yantra is not a perfect magic square (numbers are used twice), and the numbers seem to be arranged in a haphazard manner. This is not the case. Each number has been carefully selected and positioned according to numerology to create the maximum power from the talisman.

72	81	33	42
98	82	9	11
25	37	49	50
45	27	9	1

appendix

e

magical alphabets

Theban

A	𝓎		N	𝓎ₕ
B	𝓏		O	𝓂
C	𝓂		P	𝓂
D	𝓂		Q	𝓏
E	𝓂		R	𝓂
F	𝓂		S	𝓎
G	𝓋		T	𝓏
H	𝓎		U	𝓅
I	𝓋		V	𝓅
J	𝓏		W	𝓅𝓅
K	𝓒		X	𝓋
L	𝓎		Y	𝓏
M	𝓏		Z	𝓂

The Alphabet of the Magi

A	⌘	N	Ɣ
B	♈	O	▯
C	⊞	P	✗
D	⊓	Q	▯
E	♈	R	∨
F	♯	S	✳
G	℈	T	⋀⋁
H	ℵ	U	⋀
I	⌒	V	⋀
J	⌒	W	⋀⋀
K	⊃	X	‡
L	⌣	Y	⋏
M	ℸ	Z	⋁

Note: Also known as Malachim.

appendix

suggested reading

Agrippa, Henry Cornelius. *Three Books of Occult Philosophy*. Edited and annotated by Donald Tyson. St. Paul, MN: Llewellyn Publications, 1993.

Andrews, Carol. *Amulets of Ancient Egypt*. London: British Museum Press, 1994.

Barrett, Francis. *The Magus*. London: Lackington, Allen, and Co., 1801. Reprint, Wellingborough, U.K.: Aquarian Press, 1989.

Brier, Bob. *Ancient Egyptian Magic*. New York: William Morrow, 1981.

Brown, Richard S. *Ancient Astrological Gemstones and Talismans*. Bangkok, Thailand: A.G.T., 1995.

Budge, E. A. Wallis. *Amulets and Superstitions*. London: Oxford Univ. Press, 1930.

Farrell, Nick. *Making Talismans: Living Entities of Power.* St. Paul, MN: Llewellyn Publications, 2001.

González-Wippler. *The Complete Book of Amulets and Talismans.* St. Paul, MN: Llewellyn Publications, 1991.

Goodman, Frederick. *Magic Symbols.* London: Brian Trodd Publishing House, 1989.

Harris, Eleanor L. *Ancient Egyptian Divination and Magic.* York Beach, ME: Samuel Weiser, 1998.

Hartford, Bob. *The Pocket Encyclopedia of Lucky Charms.* Surry Hills, Australia: Page Publications, n.d.

Holbeche, Soozi. *The Power of Gems and Crystals.* London: Judy Piatkus, 1989.

Keyte, Geoffrey. *The Healing Crystal.* London: Blandford Press, 1989.

Küntz, Darcy, ed. *The Black Pullet.* Edmonds, WA: Holmes Publishing Group, 1999. First published 1880.

Kunz, George Frederick. *The Curious Lore of Precious Stones.* Philadelphia, PA: J. B. Lippincott Company, 1913.

Lippman, Deborah and Colin, Paul. *How to Make Amulets, Charms and Talismans*. New York: M. Evans, 1974.

Logan, Jo. *The Prediction Book of Amulets and Talismans*. Poole, U.K.: Javelin Books, 1986.

Nelson, Felicitas H. *Talismans and Amulets of the World*. New York: Sterling Publishing, 2000.

Ophiel. *The Art and Practice of Talismanic Magic*. York Beach, ME: Samuel Weiser, 1979.

Pajeon, Kala and Ketz. *The Talisman Magic Workbook*. New York: Citadel Press, 1993.

Pelton, Robert. *Voodoo Charms and Talismans*. Plainview, NY: Original Publications, 1997.

Regardie, Israel. *How to Make and Use Talismans*. New York: Samuel Weiser, 1972.

Schouten, Dr. J. *The Pentagram as a Medical Symbol*. Nieuwkoop, Netherlands: De Graaf, 1968.

Skelton, Robin. *The Magical Practice of Talismans*. Victoria, Canada: Beach Holme, 1991.

Smith, G.F. Herbert. *Gemstones*. London: Methuen, 1912.

Sorar A. L. *Western Mandalas of Transformation*. St. Paul, MN: Llewellyn Publications, 1995.

Thomas, William and Pavitt, Kate. *The Book of Talismans, Amulets and Zodiacal Gems.* Reprint, Edmonds, WA: Holmes Publishing Group, n.d.

Thompson, C. J. S. *Amulets, Talismans and Charms.* Reprint, Edmonds, WA: Holmes Publishing Group, n.d.

Vinci, Leo. *Talismans, Amulets and Charms.* London: Regency Press, 1977.

Weinstein, Michael. *The World of Jewel Stones.* London: Sir Isaac Pitman and Sons, 1959.

Whitcomb, Bill. *The Magician's Reflection.* St. Paul, MN: Llewellyn Publications, 1999.

notes

Introduction

1. A. Flinder, *Secrets of the Bible Seas* (London: Severn House, 1985), 101.

2. L. Pauwels and J. Bergier quoted René Alleau in *The Dawn of Magic* (London: Anthony Gibbs and Phillips, 1963), 43.

3. P. James and N. Thorpe, *Ancient Inventions* (London: Michael O'Mara Books, 1995), 387.

4. G. Majno, *The Healing Hand* (Harvard Univ. Press, 1975).

5. Joseph Needham, *Science and Civilisation in China*, (Cambridge Univ. Press, 1954), 2:192-193.

Chapter One

1. Harvey Day, *Occult Illustrated Dictionary* (London: Kaye and Ward, 1975), 129.

Chapter Two

1. Carol Andrews, Amulets of Ancient Egypt (London: British Museum Press, 1994), 6.

2. E. A. Wallis Budge, *Amulets and Superstitions* (Oxford: Oxford Univ. Press, 1930), xxvii.

3. C. J. S. Thompson, *Amulets, Talismans and Charms* (Edmonds, WA: Holmes Publishing Group, n.d.), 5-6.

4. R. Brasch, *The Supernatural and You!* (Stanmore, Australia: Cassell Australia, 1976), 143.

5. William Smith, *A Dictionary of Greek and Roman Antiquities* (London: John Murray, 1875), 521.

6. Carole Potter, *Knock on Wood and Other Superstitions* (New York: Sammis Publishing, 1983), 72-73.

7. Jean Patterson and Arzu Aghayeva, "The Evil Eye: Staving Off Harm–With a Visit to the Open Market," *Azerbaijan International*, Autumn 2000, 8.

8. George Frederick Kuntz, *The Curious Lore of Precious Stones* (Philadelphia, PA: Lippincott, 1913) 139.

9. Kuntz, Curious Lore, (see note 8), 137.

10. Migene González–Wippler, The Complete Book of Amulets and Talismans (St. Paul, MN: Llewellyn Publications, 1991), 174.

11. Leo Vinci, *Talismans, Amulets and Charms* (London and New York: Regency Press, 1977), 34.

12. Budge, *Amulets* (see note 2), 30.

13. Rachel Noeman, "Citizens Still Wary of 'Evil Eye' Power," *Middle East Times*, August 4th, 2001.

14. E. W. Lane, *Manners and Customs of the Modern Egyptians* (London: 1836), 243.

15. Leonard R. N. Ashley, *The Complete Book of Spells, Curses and Magical Recipes* (New York: Barricade Books, 1997), 161.

16. Brasch, *Supernatural* (see note 4), 146.

17. Alan Dundes, ed., *The Evil Eye: A Folklore Casebook* (New York: Garland Publishing, 1981).

18. Richard Webster, *Omens, Oghams and Oracles* (St. Paul, MN: Llewellyn Publications, 1995), 40.

19. Ernest Busenbark, *Symbols, Sex, and the Stars in Popular Belief* (New York: The Truth Seeker Company, 1949), 144.

20. Busenbark, *Symbols* (see note 19), 149-150.

21. Andrew D. White, *History of the Warfare of Science with Theology* (1897; repr, Chicago: Chicago Univ. Press, 1997) 1:343.

22. George Frederick Kunz, *The Magic of Jewels and Charms* (Philadelphia: J. B. Lippincott, 1915), 342.

23. Budge, *Amulets* (see note 2), 315.

24. Potter, *Knock on Wood,* (see note 6), 112.

25. Kunz, *Magic* (see note 22), 337-338.

Chapter 3

1. Robin Skelton, *The Magical Practice of Talismans* (Victoria, British Columbia: Beach Holme Publishers, 1991), 16.

2. Doreen Valiente, *Natural Magic* (Custer, WA: Phoenix Publishing, 1975), 75.

3. Albertus Magnus (attributed), *Secrets Merveilleux de la Magie Naturelle et Cabalistique du Petit Albert*, (Lyons, France: 1668).

4. Pierre de Scudalupis, *Sympathia septem metallorum* (Paris, 1610).

5. Arthur Edward Waite, *The Occult Sciences* (Secaucus, NJ: Univ. Books, 1974), 111.

6. Anonymous, *The Encyclopedia of Occult Sciences* (New York: Tudor Publishing, 1939), 417.

Chapter Four

1. Thompson, *Amulets* (see chap. 2, n. 3), 11-15.

2. Francis Barrett, *The Magus* (London: Lackington, Allen, 1801), 30.

3. Emily Gwathmey, *Lots of Luck: Legend and Lore of Good Fortune* (Santa Monica, CA: Angel City Press, 1994), 14.

4. Richard Webster, *Is Your Pet Psychic?* (St. Paul, MN: Llewellyn Publications, 2002), 15-33.

5. Potter, *Knock on Wood*, 86 (see chap. 2, n. 6).

6. Budge, *Amulets*, 468 (see chap. 2, n. 2).

7. Thompson, *Amulets* (see chap. 2, n. 3), 16-17.

8. W. Eberhard, *The Local Cultures of South and East China* (Leiden: E. J. Brill, 1968), 132.

9. Vinci, *Talismans* (see chap. 2, n. 11), 45.

10. Iona and Peter Opie, eds., *The Oxford Dictionary of Nursery Rhymes* (Oxford: Oxford Univ. Press, 1952), 263-264.

11. Budge, *Amulets* (see chap. 2, n. 2), 490.

12. Webster, *Omens* (see chap. 2, n. 18), 22-23.

13. Bob Hartford, *The Pocket Encyclopaedia of Lucky Charms* (Surry Hills, Australia: Page Publications, n.d.), 42.

14. Michael Weinstein, *The World of Jewel Stones* (London: Sir Isaac Pitman and Son, 1959), 71.

15. Kunz, *Curious Lore* (see chap. 2, n. 8), 349.

16. Vinci, *Talismans* (see chap. 2, n. 11), 50-51.

17. Gwathmey, *Lots of Luck* (see chap. 4, n. 3), 32.

18. Andrews, *Amulets* (see chap. 2, n. 1), 50.

19. Brasch, *Supernatural* (see chap. 2, n. 4), 203.

20. Budge, *Amulets* (see chp. 2, n. 2), 134.

Chapter Five

1. Richard Webster, *Pendulum Magic for Beginners* (St. Paul, MN: Llewellyn Publications, 2002), 179-200; for further info. on the kahuna system.

2. Thompson, *Amulets* (see chap. 2, n. 3), 22.

3. Andrews, *Amulets* (see chap. 2, n. 1), 106.

Chapter Six

1. Joan Evans, *Magical Jewels of the Middle Ages and the Renaissance* (Oxford: Oxford Univ. Press, 1922), 13.

2. Weinstein, *World of Jewel* (see chap. 4, n. 14), 3.

3. Geoffrey Keyte, *The Healing Crystal: A Practical Handbook* (London: Blandford, 1989), 15.

4. Ibid., 7.

5. Soozi Holbeche, *The Power of Gems and Crystals* (London: Judy Piatkus, 1989), 21.

6. Thompson, *Amulets* (see chap. 2, n. 3), 8.

7. Cornelia M. Parkinson, *Gem Magic* (New York: Fawcett Columbine, 1988), 30.

8. Carol Clark, *Tropical Gemstones of Malaysia and Southeast Asia* (Hong Kong: Periplus Editions, 1998), 7.

9. Richard S. Brown, *Ancient Astrological Gemstones and Talismans* (Bangkok, Thailand: A.G.T. Limited, 1995), 31.

10. Clark, *Tropical* (see note 8), 56.

Chapter Seven

1. Richard Webster, *Talisman Magic* (St. Paul, MN: Llewellyn Publications, 1995), xiii.

2. Jim Moran, *The Wonders of Magic Squares* (New York: Vintage Books, 1982), 5.

3. Paul Carus, intro. to *Magic Squares and Cubes,* ed. W.S. Andrews, (Chicago: Open Court, 1917), vii-viii.

4. David Allen Hulse, *The Key of It All: An Encyclopedic Guide to the Sacred Languages and Magickal Systems of the World,* Vol. 2, The Western Mysteries (St. Paul, MN: Llewellyn Publications, 1994), lix.

5. Nigel Pennick, *The Secret Lore of Runes and Other Ancient Alphabets* (London: Rider and Company, 1991), 204.

6. S. L. MacGregor Mathers, trans., *The Book of the Sacred Magic of Abramelin the Mage* (London: John M. Watkins, 1900; repr. New York: Dover Publications, 1975).

Appendix C

1. William Thomas and Kate Pavitt, *The Book of Talismans, Amulets and Zodiacal Gems,* 3rd ed. (1914; repr., Kila, MT: Kessinger Publishing Company, n.d.), 141.

2. Ibid., 210.

index

243

index

244

index